Jack London

The People to Know Series

Neil Armstrong
*The First Man
on the Moon*
0-89490-828-6

Isaac Asimov
*Master of
Science Fiction*
0-7660-1031-7

Robert Ballard
*Oceanographer Who
Discovered the* Titanic
0-7660-1147-X

Willa Cather
Writer of the Prairie
0-89490-980-0

Bill Clinton
*United States
President*
0-89490-437-X

Hillary Rodham Clinton
Activist First Lady
0-89490-583-X

Bill Cosby
Actor and Comedian
0-89490-548-1

Walt Disney
*Creator of
Mickey Mouse*
0-89490-694-1

Bob Dole
Legendary Senator
0-89490-825-1

Marian Wright Edelman
*Fighting for
Children's Rights*
0-89490-623-2

Bill Gates
*Billionaire
Computer Genius*
0-89490-824-3

Jane Goodall
Protector of Chimpanzees
0-89490-827-8

Al Gore
*Leader for the
New Millennium*
0-7660-1232-8

Tipper Gore
*Activist, Author,
Photographer*
0-7660-1142-9

Ernest Hemingway
Writer and Adventurer
0-89490-979-7

Ron Howard
*Child Star &
Hollywood Director*
0-89490-981-9

John F. Kennedy
*President of the
New Frontier*
0-89490-693-3

John Lennon
The Beatles and Beyond
0-89490-702-6

Maya Lin
Architect and Artist
0-89490-499-X

Jack London
*A Writer's
Adventurous Life*
0-7660-1144-5

Barbara McClintock
*Nobel Prize
Geneticist*
0-89490-983-5

Christopher Reeve
*Hollywood's Man
of Courage*
0-7660-1149-6

Ann Richards
*Politician, Feminist,
Survivor*
0-89490-497-3

Sally Ride
*First American Woman
in Space*
0-89490-829-4

Will Rogers
*Cowboy
Philosopher*
0-89490-695-X

Franklin D. Roosevelt
*The Four-Term
President*
0-89490-696-8

Steven Spielberg
*Hollywood
Filmmaker*
0-89490-697-6

Martha Stewart
*Successful
Businesswoman*
0-89490-984-3

Amy Tan
Author of
The Joy Luck Club
0-89490-699-2

Alice Walker
Author of
The Color Purple
0-89490-620-8

Simon Wiesenthal
*Tracking Down
Nazi Criminals*
0-89490-830-8

Frank Lloyd Wright
*Visionary
Architect*
0-7660-1032-5

People to Know

Jack London

A Writer's Adventurous Life

Elaine Slivinski Lisandrelli

Enslow Publishers, Inc.

40 Industrial Road   PO Box 38
Box 398   Aldershot
Berkeley Heights, NJ 07922   Hants GU12 6BP
USA   UK

http://www.enslow.com

For Chet and Geneva Sharek,
my dear uncle and aunt, with love and gratitude

Library of Congress Cataloging-in-Publication Data

Lisandrelli, Elaine Slivinski.
    Jack London : a writer's adventurous life / Elaine Slivinski Lisandrelli.
        p. cm. — (People to know)
    Includes bibliographical references and index.
    Summary: Describes the childhood, travel, adventures, and writing career of the
man who wrote "The Call of the Wild" and "White Fang."
    ISBN 0-7660-1144-5
    1. London, Jack, 1876–1916—Juvenile literature. 2. Authors, American—
20th century—Biography—Juvenile literature. 3. Adventure and adventurers—
United States—Biography—Juvenile literature. [1. London, Jack, 1876–1916.
2. Authors, American.] I. Title. II. Series.
PS3523.046Z687   1999
813'.52—dc21
[b]   98-50565
                                                                  CIP
                                                                   AC
Printed in the United States of America

10 9 8 7 6 5 4 3 2 1

To Our Readers:
All Internet addresses in this book were active and appropriate when we went to press.
Any comments or suggestions can be sent by e-mail to Comments@enslow.com or to
the address on the back cover.

Illustration Credits:
© California State Parks, Jack London Collection, pp. 41, 74, 77, 83, 86, 90,
96, 104; Carl A. Lisandrelli, Moosic, Pennsylvania, pp. 93, 98, 101, 106,
107, 124; Courtesy Oakland Public Library, Oakland History Room, pp. 13,
17, 21, 23, 26, 31, 43, 60, 68; Enslow Publishers, Inc., p. 54; This item (JLP
463, Album 25 #03150) is reproduced by permission of the Huntington
Library, San Marino, California, p. 80.

Cover Illustration:
Courtesy Oakland Public Library, Oakland History Room

Acknowledgments

My deepest gratitude goes to the following individuals for their kindness, encouragement, and support:

I. Milo Shepard, Jack London's great-nephew and trustee of the estate of Irving Shepard, for the opportunity to meet with him and for his kind correspondence and generous permission to examine primary sources and original photographs.

Winnie Kingman of the Jack London Research Center, who was most gracious to me during my research. She carries on the outstanding work begun by her late husband, Russ Kingman.

Greg Hayes of Jack London State Historic Park, who gave a most informative tour.

Glenn Burch, State Historian for the California State Parks in Sonoma, for his assistance with photographs.

Kathleen Leles DiGiovanni of the Oakland Public Library and Richard Ogar of the Bancroft Library at the University of California, Berkeley, who were patient with my inquiries.

Sue Hodson, curator of Literary Manuscripts at the Huntington Library in San Marino, California, who went out of her way to assist me during this project.

All who read my manuscript and offered insightful critiques, including Jack London scholars Earle Labor, Susan Nuernberg, and Dennis Hensley; Gladys Greene and Winnie Kingman of the Jack London Research Center; and members of my writers' group:

Susan Campbell Bartoletti, Lisa Rowe Fraustino, Anna Grossnickle Hines, Mary Joyce Love, and Laura Lee Wren.

My relatives in California, who were so gracious to me during the summer of my research: my uncle and aunt, Chet and Geneva Sharek; my cousins Ron Sharek and R.C. Sharek; Steve and Nancy Sharek; Gregg, Sue, Taylor, and Alana Magaziner; and Michael, Monica, and Maxwell Dergosits, and my brother and sister-in-law, Dennis and Michele Slivinski.

My family and friends for their kindness, especially my parents, Leo and Gabriella Sharek Slivinski, and my husband, Carl. I'm grateful he accompanied me on my journey to London's beautiful "Valley of the Moon."

Contents

"Thirty Days"

On a June afternoon in 1894, eighteen-year-old Jack London rode into Niagara Falls in a stuffy boxcar. After the train jerked to a halt, he headed for the famous falls. This handsome, five-foot-seven adventurer watched in awe as the water fell more than 150 feet with a tremendous roar. Hours later moonlight illuminated the continuous rush of water, hypnotizing him. As his eyes became heavy with sleep, he did not seek a room in a hotel. Instead he flopped in a nearby field, surrounded by stars.

He awakened at sunrise eager to see the falls once more, but three men—he assumed they were hobos like himself—headed toward him. Soon he learned that the man in the middle was not a hobo, but a lawman. The lawman led Jack London away to the city jail, for in 1894 in Erie County, New York, wandering without the proper means to earn a living—being a hobo—was a crime. London was searched and his name was entered into the prison register.

Jack London and fifteen other men who had wandered about, living by begging or doing odd jobs, found themselves in a courtroom. As the judge called out each name, a hobo rose from the wooden chair. The bailiff announced the charge, "Vagrancy, Your Honor."

The judge swiftly issued the punishment: "Thirty days."

The accused sat down without a protest. This process was repeated. Within fifteen seconds, thirty days of freedom were taken away from each of the men. One of the hobos got a chance to tell his tale of hardship, but his story did not change the judge's mind.

When the time came for the charge against Jack London, he protested and demanded a jury trial.

"Thirty days," responded the irate judge.

London continued to speak out, but the judge's patience wore thin, and he told the young man accused of vagrancy, "Shut up!"[1]

The bailiff forced a disillusioned London to sit down. Questions ran through London's mind: Why am I not allowed to plead guilty or not guilty? Why am I not allowed to tell my story? What has happened to an American's right to trial by jury?[2]

The system gave Jack London harsh answers: He could *not* have an attorney, and he could *not* have a second chance. The Erie County Penitentiary became London's address. His thick brown hair was shaved, and he wore an oversized prison shirt and a striped coat and trousers.

For the next thirty days, London ate little more than bread and water. He traded some bread for other items, including a ration of meat, a paperback novel, and an occasional newspaper. Hundreds of bedbugs infested his cell, screams and howls from prisoners throwing violent fits invaded his space, and guards used force against prisoners. "The things I saw there gave me a terrible scare," he later stated.[3]

In that Erie County Penitentiary he witnessed brutality that he would never fully reveal. "I saw with my own eyes, there in that prison, things unbelievable and monstrous," he related in *The Road*.[4]

After Jack London's jail term officially ended on July 29, 1894, he hopped another train. Before he returned home to Oakland, California, in late fall, he had traveled thousands of miles, many of them on the rods underneath railcars or in empty boxcars. Once he slept in a flatcar with lumber, making an old newspaper his pillow. He listened intently to educated tramps lecture on park benches, arguing about philosophy, science, and the economy. He had time to listen to the sad stories of others. He had time to think about where he was headed in his own life.

♦ ♦ ♦

The degrading prison experience and his travels as a hobo proved to be a turning point in the life of Jack

London.[5] "I found myself looking upon life from a new and totally different angle," he later said.[6] He became more attuned to the plight of the poor. He saw that working-class people had little power and very few rights. He realized that an education could get him out of a life of poverty.[7] Years later he recalled, "I resolved to sell no more muscle, and to become a vendor of brains. Then began a frantic pursuit of knowledge. I returned to California and opened the books."[8]

After years of unbelievable struggle, Jack London gained recognition as one of the world's best-loved writers. He brought new themes into literature and captivated readers with his realistic details. In the early 1900s, magazine readers saw the name Jack London almost every month in an issue of some popular magazine. Although he would be best known for *The Call of the Wild*, which author Carl Sandburg described as "the greatest dog story ever written," London created fifty other books, two hundred short stories, and four hundred nonfiction selections on a wide range of topics.[9] Some have been translated into nearly ninety languages. He was also a man who deeply loved the land and the sea. He formulated a philosophy that led him through many hard times, quiet explorations, and great adventures. He wrote:

> *I would rather be ashes than dust!*
> *I would rather*
> > *that my spark should burn out in a brilliant blaze*
> > *than it should be stifled by dryrot.*
> *I would rather be a superb meteor,*

After years of unbelievable struggle, Jack London would triumph
as one of the world's best-loved writers.

every atom of me in magnificent glow,
than a sleepy and permanent planet.
The proper function of man is to live, not to exist.
I shall not waste my days in trying to prolong them.
I shall use my time.[10]

Jack London's life was as fascinating as any story-teller could have created. In his forty years on this planet, he composed a body of literary work that has survived the test of time. Decades after his death, the brightness of this literary meteor still captivates new generations of readers.

Early Lessons

On January 12, 1876, the same year the United States celebrated its one-hundredth birthday, Flora Wellman gave birth to a son. She named him John Griffith Chaney, although the boy's father was not at her side. In fact, William H. Chaney, who had lived with Flora for one year, denied he was the boy's father. He even advised her to have an abortion when he first learned she was pregnant. She refused, and several months before the baby's birth, Chaney left her. She moved in with friends.

When Wellman was younger, a severe fever had stunted her growth and damaged her hair and eyesight. Now, after the baby's birth, she became especially weak and had difficulty nursing her new son. Her doctor suggested she ask for help from Virginia Prentiss, an African-American woman whose baby had recently died in childbirth. Prentiss nursed Wellman's baby for eight months. The baby grew to love Prentiss very much, and later he affectionately called her "Mammy Jennie."

Wellman had no money to pay Virginia Prentiss, so she made shirts for Prentiss's husband, Alonzo. These well-made shirts got the attention of Alonzo's boss, a carpenter named John London. One day he visited Wellman to order a shirt from her. Soon John and Flora married, and Flora renamed her eight-month-old son John Griffith London. The boy answered to the name "Johnny" until he selected Jack on his own when he entered the Cole Grammar School.

Jack's stepfather, John London, loved Jack as his own son. Jack returned that love, and he referred to London as his father. John London was a widower who had fought in the Union Army during the Civil War. He had headed west after his son Charles was injured in the chest playing baseball. A doctor advised that the only hope for the boy's recovery would be in California. John London made arrangements to have others care for his older children and came to California with Charles and his two daughters, Eliza and Ida. Charles never recovered from his injury, dying eleven days after their arrival in California.

After John married Flora, John's daughter Eliza enjoyed wheeling her new baby brother, "Johnny," in his carriage. They formed a warm relationship and forever remained close.

Throughout Jack's childhood, the family had

Jack London's parents

John London, *stepfather*	*Flora Wellman London,* *mother*

numerous addresses, including the farm and city sections of the San Francisco Bay area. They moved almost twenty times during the first thirteen years of Jack's life, each time hoping the move would bring financial security. Flora London earned money giving piano lessons, sewing, and taking in boarders. John London was a hard worker who tried numerous jobs, including growing vegetables and operating a chicken ranch. He knew one business failure after another. Young Jack, painfully aware of these financial struggles, worked odd jobs whenever he could.

Jack's mother, Flora, cooked meals, made his clothing, and visited his school to be sure his teacher was giving him enough attention, but she did not show her son much outward affection. She threw temper tantrums and often held séances in which she said she communicated with the spirits of the dead. These activities frightened young Jack. When things went wrong, his father would always lay his hand over Jack's head and say, "There, there, sonny."[1]

Father and son shared some peaceful times on and near the water: In an inlet lying between Oakland and Alameda, they dug for clams in the cool mud and fished for flounder and rock cod. Later Jack London would say of his stepfather, "My father was the best man I have ever known."[2]

When Jack was five, he lugged a tin pail of beer to his father working in the fields. He was anxious to try this liquid that grown-ups drank. He buried his face in the foam, but he hated the taste. The delicious liquid must be hiding under the foam, he thought.[3] He put his face deeper and drank more and more, still not enjoying it. He could not risk having his father notice that some beer was missing, so Jack took a stick and mixed the remains until white bubbles turned to foamy layers. John London never suspected anything was wrong, but the beer had made young Jack dizzy. As he tried to walk beside the horses pulling his father's plow, he was almost trampled. His father halted the plow just in time to save him, then carried him in his arms to some nearby trees to sleep off the effects of the beer. Jack remembered, "My condition was like that of one who had gone through a battle with poison. In truth I had been poisoned."[4]

Jack fondly remembered the saloons of San

Francisco where he often went with his father, not for the beer but for other special treats. While his father had a few mugs of beer, young Jack enjoyed strange breads and soda crackers, cheeses, sausages, and sardines that were not a part of the usual London dinner table. He remembered a bartender mixing him a nonalcoholic drink of sweet red-colored syrup and soda water and not charging his father for it. "It was the barkeeper's treat, and he became my ideal of a good, kind man. . . . He and my father talked long, and I sipped my sweet drink and worshipped him. And for years afterwards I worshipped the memory of him."[5]

Even before he was enrolled as a student, Jack accompanied his sister Eliza to school. By age five he was reading and writing. He completed eighth grade at the Cole Grammar School, but like many other children during that time, he did not go on to high school.

In school Jack learned his lessons quickly. Although he was bashful when he had to recite a Christmas poem, his teachers thought him bold when he asked a lot of questions. To find answers to his many questions, he read books. He remembered, "I read everything, but principally history and adventure, and all the old travels and voyages. I read mornings, afternoons and nights. I read in bed, I read at table, I read as I walked to and from school, and I read at recess while the other boys were playing."[6]

Books were a treasure to Jack. When he was eight years old, he read a book called *Signa* by Ouida. He identified with Signa, the Italian peasant child who longed for fame. Signa's dreams made Jack want to dream, too. "When I read it, I was a little peasant on a poor California ranch. Reading the story, my narrowhill-horizon was pushed back, and all the world was made possible if I would dare it."[7] Since the last forty pages of his copy were missing, he did not read the tragic ending until he was an adult.

Young Jack London read Washington Irving's *Alhambra* over and over. As part of his fantasy world, he created a little redbrick Alhambra from discarded bricks of a fallen chimney. He built towers and terraces and arcades and labeled these sections with school chalk. How proud he was of his Alhambra! How hurt he was when a well-dressed visitor to his parents made fun of his creation! The hurt deepened when this man stole Jack's beloved copy of *Alhambra* and hid it in the cellar crawl space. Furiously, Jack fumbled through darkness and spider webs searching until he found it.

When the Londons moved back to Oakland in 1886, librarian Ina Coolbrith remembered that Jack was hungry for books. London would admire Miss Coolbrith his whole life through. Shortly before his thirty-first birthday, he wrote her a letter remembering that special time:

> *Do you know you were the first one who ever complimented me on my choice of reading matter? Nobody at home bothered their heads over what I read. I was an eager, thirsty, hungry little kid—and one day at the library I drew out a volume on Pizzaro in Peru (I was ten years old). You got the book and stamped it for me; and as you handed it*

to me you praised me for reading books of that nature.

Proud! If you only knew how proud your words made me! For I thought a great deal of you. You were a goddess to me.[8]

Jack London loved books and he loved boats. Each offered him adventure, hope, and peace. He learned to sail on San Francisco Bay and enjoyed boating and fishing in an estuary lying between Oakland and Alameda. Perch, rock cod, and striped bass dangling from the end of his hook pleased him. The ebb and flow of the tides rocking his boat, the wind blowing his brown curls back, and the salt air rippling the cotton sails were all wonders to him. He loved the sounds of seals and sea lions and the warmth of the sun on his face.

Librarian Ina Coolbrith encouraged young Jack London's interest in reading.

There was never enough time for the things that young Jack wanted to do. At age ten Jack was on the streets selling newspapers. He got up at three to carry the morning papers, then he went to school. When school was over, he carried the evening papers. On Saturday he worked on the ice wagon. On Sunday he set up pins in a bowling alley. He knew his family needed money. "I turned over every cent and went dressed like a scarecrow," he remembered.[9]

Trading and collecting also filled his days. He hunted and labeled bird eggs. He saved marbles that he won in games played on the street or in the schoolyard. He traded "extra" newspapers from his paper route for series cards and posters that came in cigarette packages, including categories like Great Race Horses, Champion Prize Fighters, and Women of All Nations. Other boys trusted him to sell their collections of bottles, rags, grain sacks, old iron, and five-gallon oil cans for the best price. He earned a commission for his clever ways.

When he was fifteen, he worked at an Oakland cannery, which was set up in an unsanitary old stable. Pickles, tomatoes, peaches, berries, and corn went into shiny tin cans and jars, but so did the dust that often blew through the barn and into the cannery. It was not uncommon for a young worker to lose a finger in one of the machines. At that time there were no laws to prevent child labor or the dangerous conditions of the workplace. For ten cents an hour, boys and girls worked side by side, standing over the same machine for eighteen to twenty hours at a time. Once Jack worked at his machine for thirty-six hours

In 1886, ten-year-old Jack, with his dog, Rollo, had this picture taken as a gift for his sister Eliza.

in a row. "I asked myself if this were the meaning of life—to be a workbeast. I knew no horse in the city of Oakland that worked the hours I worked."[10]

Amid the squalor of the cannery, Jack remembered the freedom of sailing, the wind on the bay, the sunrises and sunsets that he was never able to see anymore, and the salt water that touched his skin. He needed adventure. He knew he had to get away.[11]

He was fifteen when he bought a boat, the *Razzle Dazzle*, from a fifty-year-old oyster pirate known as "French Frank." Jack's beloved Mammy Jennie lent him the $300 he needed. The deal was finalized at Heinold's First and Last Chance Saloon, where Jack used to snack, study, and sweep floors. Now he was officially an oyster pirate, one of the small-boat owners who raided the oyster beds at night and sold their stolen goods to San Francisco market and saloon owners. Some of the police and the public sympathized with the oyster pirates because many of the oyster beds were controlled by the hated Southern Pacific Railroad, which had leased the beds to oyster growers and caused prices to be very high.[12]

On his first raid Jack made as much money as he had earned in three months at the cannery. Every time he and his mates went on a raid, they risked ending up in state prison, but Jack reasoned: "I wanted to be where the winds of adventure blew. And the winds of adventure blew the oyster pirate sloops up and down San Francisco Bay. . . . The men in stripes worked a shorter day than I at my machine. And there was vastly more romance in being an oyster pirate or a convict than in being a machine slave."[13]

These firsthand experiences as an oyster pirate served Jack London well in later years. They helped him create accurate descriptions in *The Cruise of the Dazzler*:

> *The boys laid hold of the line and hove in the dredge. The net was full of mud and slime and small oysters, with here and there a large one. This mess they dumped on the deck and picked over while the dredge was dragging again. The large oysters they threw into the cockpit, and shoveled the rubbish overboard. There was no rest, for by this time the other dredge required emptying. And when this was done and the oysters sorted, both dredges had to be hauled aboard.*[14]

Soon Jack sent word home to his mother to call the neighborhood boys together and give them all the "treasures" that he had collected—marbles, posters, cards. He remembered, "I was a man now, and I made a clean sweep of everything that bound me to my boyhood."[15]

Jack London's pirating buddies admired his skill, daring, and charm and gave him the title "Prince of the Oyster Pirates." London did not like the taste of beer, but drinking was a normal part of life on the waterfront in those days, and to win acceptance—to become, as he said, "a man among men"—he did his share of drinking.[16] The thrifty Jack London soon became the spender, buying drinks for the men he met on the waterfront. Later, he would admit in his book *John Barleycorn* (John Barleycorn is another name for alcohol) that his drinking was "sordid and silly."[17]

As a teenager he drank in public, but he preferred candy. "I would go up to the Free Library, exchange my books, buy a quarter's worth of all sorts of candy that chewed and lasted, sneak aboard the *Razzle Dazzle*, lock myself in the cabin, go to bed, and lie there long hours of bliss, reading and chewing candy. . . . Dollars and dollars, across the bar, couldn't buy the satisfaction that twenty-five cents did in a candy store."[18]

Jack experienced some good times as an oyster pirate and learned a great deal about the waterways

The Cole Grammar School Class of 1887, with London's photo circled. Like many children of his time, Jack did not go on to high school after completing eighth grade. He went to work, but soon he heard the call of the sea—and adventure.

and the waterfront. But he still worried that he could end up in jail for being one.[19]

In 1892 London switched to the other side and became a deputy patrolman for the California Fish Patrol. Now he had the authority to arrest those who broke the fishing laws. The Fish Patrol battled lawbreakers, including Chinese shrimp catchers and fishermen who trapped sturgeon in a cruel manner, used illegal nets, or ignored the ban on setting a net to catch salmon between sundown Saturday night and sunup Monday morning.

London received a percentage of the fines imposed upon the convicted violators and any rewards that might have been offered. He did not make as much money as an oyster pirate, but this was honest work. He rode a patrol ship, often keeping four-hour watches in the middle of the night. "My only weapon on duty was a steel table-fork, but I felt fearless and a man when I climbed over the side of a boat to arrest some marauder."[20]

Even though London was on the side of the law, he had the ability to see the struggle of those who tried to make a living. In *Tales of the Fish Patrol*, London wrote of their pursuit of the Greek fishermen:

> *We menaced their lives, or their living, which is the same thing, in many ways. We confiscated illegal traps and nets, the materials of which had cost them considerable sums and the making of which required weeks of labor. We prevented them from catching fish at many times and seasons, which was equivalent to preventing them from making as good a living as they might have made had we not been in existence.*

> *And when we captured them, they were brought into the courts of law, where heavy cash fines were collected from them. As a result, they hated us vindictively. As the dog is the natural enemy of the cat, the snake of man, so were we of the fish patrol the natural enemies of the fishermen.*[21]

London's new companions, the members of the Fish Patrol, drank even more than the oyster pirates. It was still the waterfront, and to be a part of it, London felt he had to drink. He viewed himself as "a pretty tough individual in a group of pretty tough men; and I drank because these men drank and because I had to make good with them."[22] One night London became so drunk he fell overboard and was borne away by a current. At some point during his four hours in the cold water, he hoped he would drown. As the liquor wore off, he wanted to live. "And I knew fear. I was sober now, and I didn't want to die. I discovered scores of reasons for living."[23] Fortunately, a Greek salmon fisherman rescued him from the strong riptides that were pulling him under.

Jack London came to the realization that men did violent and irrational things when they were drunk. He knew he must find a way out of this environment. There was another world out there to explore.[24]

On January 20, 1893, eight days after his seventeenth birthday, he signed on with the *Sophia Sutherland*, a three-topmast sealing schooner bound on a voyage to the coast of Japan.

Adventure by Sea, Adventure by Land

At seventeen, Jack London was the youngest crew member on the deep-sea vessel called the *Sophia Sutherland*. The experienced sailors heckled him, but he convinced them he was a worthy sailor.

London was the first of the watch to go on deck, and one of the last to go below. He never left a sheet or tackle for someone else to coil over a pin. He willingly ran aloft when topsail sheets and tacks were shifted or when topsails were set or taken in.[1] If pressed to fight, he was ready. Once during a typhoon London alone steered the *Sophia Sutherland*, a hundred tons of wood and iron, as she stove through the brutal foam-capped waves. Later he credited his excellent work habits to experiences at sea: "The discipline I had as a sailor had full effect on me."[2]

Within fifty-one days of departure, they reached the Bonin Islands (Ogasawara Islands), five hundred miles southeast of Japan. London relished the scent of tropical fruit and flowers and coco-palms. Japanese sampans and native canoes surrounded the *Sophia Sutherland* when she rested in Bonin for ten days. Then the race for the sealing grounds began.

In the waters of the North Pacific Ocean, where the fog hides the sun for a week at a time, the crew of the *Sophia Sutherland* spent one hundred days hunting seal herds along the northern coasts of Japan to the Bering Sea. They slaughtered seals, skinned them, and stripped meat and blubber from the slimy hides. London remembered, "The deck was a slaughter-house, week in and week out."[3] The men were careful not to damage the fur that eventually would be made into valuable coats.

Completing their seal mission, they began their thirty-seven-day return voyage. They sailed south to Yokohama, Japan, then to California by a northerly course.

Jack London had spent almost eight months of his young life on this expedition. Although he started this journey knowing how to steer "full-and-by" and "close-and-by," there he had learned to steer by compass and learned the art of fancy rope tying. London had also read many books he had taken aboard in his canvas seabag. On August 26, 1893, the *Sophia Sutherland* safely dropped anchor in San Francisco Bay.

As they touched land, London and the other crew

Young Jack London proved he was a worthy sailor on the
Sophia Sutherland.

members each had a pocketful of money. Jack bought himself some secondhand clothing and spent seventy-five cents for drinks for himself and some buddies he knew before going to sea.

While the other crew members stayed at the wharf, drinking away most of their wages, Jack London returned home. He gave the rest of his hard-earned pay to his mother and found work in a jute mill for ten cents an hour. He hated the monotony of winding the strong jute twine from a small bobbin onto a speedily moving large bobbin, but he did this work ten hours each day.

When the *San Francisco Morning Call* advertised for the best piece of descriptive writing from anyone under the age of twenty-two, Flora London encouraged her son to enter. The $25 prize sounded tempting. Jack would have to work several weeks at the jute mill to earn that much.

His mother begged him to write about his sea voyage. Although he was exhausted from his job at the jute mill and knew he needed to be up at half past five for another shift, he took an old school tablet and wrote the night through. By morning, two thousand words appeared on the papers—only half his story of the powerful typhoon he had lived through. The next night he wrote another two thousand words to complete his adventure tale. The third night, he edited his manuscript to meet the two-thousand-word contest requirement. When his mother delivered the manuscript to the editors, she said, "John has often wished he could write about what he has seen."[4]

On Sunday morning, November 12, 1893, the

winners were announced and their pictures and award-winning stories were printed in the newspaper. Seventeen-year-old Jack London, who had only completed eighth grade, had won over students from prestigious institutions like Stanford University and the University of California at Berkeley. The excellent details he included took his reader into the world of the *Sophia Sutherland.*

Even though the judges felt London's story deserved first prize, they said he made one mistake: He wrote his story in the present tense. Before printing his story, editors changed his present-tense verbs to past tense. Many people later felt that these editors destroyed the power and the charm of his story. Years after, London's daughter Joan would comment, "They blue-penciled the vivid description of the storm, the race of the small boats back to the schooner, the death of the bricklayer-sailor, slowing its tempo, robbing it of much vitality with 'wases' and 'weres' and 'hadbeens.'"[5]

The following is an excerpt from London's prize-winning story "Typhoon off the Coast of Japan" with the editorial verb changes (a copy of the original draft London wrote is unavailable):

> *It was a dry storm in the matter of rain, but the force of the wind filled the air with fine spray, which flew as high as the crosstrees and cut the face like a knife, making it impossible to see over a hundred yards ahead. The sea was a dark lead colour as with long, slow, majestic roll it was heaped up by the wind into liquid mountains of foam. The wild antics of the schooner were sickening as she forged along. She would almost stop, as though climbing a*

mountain, then rapidly rolling to right and left as she gained the summit of a huge sea, she steadied herself and paused for a moment as though affrighted at the yawning precipice before her.[6]

Pleased by winning, Jack London wrote more stories but received only rejection slips. The jute mill refused to raise his pay to a dollar and a quarter a day, so London quit. Unskilled jobs did not pay enough. London did not have the money to attend a technical school or a university, yet he felt he had to learn a skill.

With this new realization, London went to San Leandro and Haywards Electric Railway in Oakland. In the superintendent's beautiful, private office, London explained that he wanted to become an electrician. The superintendent listened intently. Then he promised London a future under one condition: London must begin on the very bottom of the ladder—he must begin as a coal heaver.

London eagerly became a coal heaver, working ten hours a day, including Sundays and holidays, with only one day off each month. He earned $30 a month, the same pay as at the jute mill, but here he learned a trade:

I was passing coal to the firemen, who shoveled it into the furnaces, where its energy was transformed into steam, which, in the engine room, was transformed into the electricity with which the electricians worked. This passing coal was surely the very beginning— unless the superintendent should take it into his head to send me to work in the mines from which the

> *coal came in order to get a complete understanding*
> *of the genesis of electricity for street railways.*[7]

Coal heaving was much harder than London had imagined. Hour after hour he filled the iron wheelbarrows with coal and trundled them into the fire room. He dripped with sweat. Coal dust coated his face. His knees trembled. His wrists swelled. When he was alone, he cried from despair.[8] He worked through lunch. He never finished before eight at night. Too tired to eat supper, he often fell asleep at the table. His mother and father helped him to his room. But Jack London was determined to learn a trade. He would not give up. He limped to work the next morning, each wrist bound with a broad leather strap.

Soon London discovered a bitter truth. One fellow worker had the courage to tell him that two men, each one paid $40 a month, had been fired, and London had been hired to do the work of both of them. London bristled at the fact that he slaved twelve to fourteen hours a day with no overtime so the company could save $50 a month. The superintendent who had seemed so concerned for his welfare never intended for him to advance. London, too proud to quit right away, remembered: "I worked on until the time came when I got in the last of the night coal by six o'clock. Then I quit the job of learning electricity by doing more than two men's work for a boy's wages, went home, and proceeded to sleep the clock around."[9]

Hard times seemed to be common for many Americans in the 1890s. There were few jobs, and they paid low wages. History books record the Panic of

1893. By the end of that troublesome year, many banks, railroad companies, and businesses had failed. A silver dollar's value had dropped to less than sixty cents. Some courageous individuals took action to protest these harsh economic conditions. One such person was businessman Jacob S. Coxey.

In 1892, Coxey asked Congress to pass a "good roads bill," through which the government would construct and improve the roads throughout the country. This would provide jobs and put more money into circulation. His bill was rejected. In 1894, Coxey led an army of the nation's unemployed to march on Washington, D.C. Individuals out of work, including miners, farmhands, shoemakers, and ironmakers, dramatized the needs of the poor by appearing in Washington. Unemployed from all over the country wanted to be a part of this industrial army, known as "Coxey's Army." Charles T. Kelly, a San Francisco printer, became the leader of the West Coast Group, numbering about fifteen hundred men. Needing escape and adventure, Jack London joined the group.

In April 1894, eighteen-year-old Jack London became a private in Company L of the Second Division of Kelly's Industrial Army. Traveling proved difficult. The railroads refused to transport Kelly's men, so the troops walked alongside wagons carrying their small quantities of food and supplies. By late April, blisters coated Jack's feet. The army made little progress, and Jack saw no point in staying on. By late May, he deserted at Hannibal, Missouri.

The main organizer of the march, Jacob S. Coxey, did arrive in Washington. Only about five hundred men, a small portion of the troops from around the country, joined him. The public greeted Coxey warmly, but the police arrested him for trespassing on the Capitol lawn. His march did not have the impact he had hoped for.

London headed on his own path to adventure. A letter from his sister Eliza awaited him in Chicago, containing $4! He bought an overcoat, hat, pants, and a shirt and had fifty cents to spend for a bed at the Salvation Army, his first real sleeping place since he left home. He visited relatives of his mother and stopped by the grounds of the World's Columbian Exposition where the famous world's fair had taken place.

As he tramped along near Niagara Falls in late June, he was arrested for vagrancy. Most of July was spent serving his thirty days in the Erie County Penitentiary. After his prison term, he again used the rails to get home. Later, in *The Road*, an account of his hobo days, London described the danger of walking on the roofs of passenger coaches on a rapidly moving train:

> *Just let him walk along the roof of a jolting, lurching car, with nothing to hold on to but the black and empty air, and when he comes to the down-curving end of the roof, all wet and slippery with dew, let him accelerate his speed so as to step across to the next roof, down curving and wet and slippery. Believe me, he will learn whether his heart is weak or his head is giddy.* [10]

While tramping, Jack London learned the technique of the short story. He talked himself out of many arrests by weaving a good tale. Many people who helped hoboes liked hearing hard-luck stories. If the story was particularly sad, some packed more food into the bag. In *The Road*, he recalls creating convincing stories at one home: "In fact with every touch I added to the picture, that kind soul gave me something also. She made up a lunch for me to carry away. She put in many boiled eggs, pepper, and salt, and other things, and a big apple."[11] One night riding in a refrigerator car, London was packed in with eighty-four men, each one with a story to tell.

Life on the road allowed Jack London to listen to hundreds of stories of adventure and many true tales of suffering. He learned how men had been fired from jobs when they became weak. He heard that when a man lost an arm or a leg on the job, the bosses asked him not to return to work.

London later claimed that his tramping experiences made him a socialist.[12] London believed that any man who longed for a better form of government than he was living under was a socialist.[13] He defined a socialist as a person who fought against social injustice—the conditions in life that were unfair.

He returned home by way of Canada, and when he became tired of the rails he worked his way as a coal stoker on the *Umatilla*. At that time, of course, he did not know that two and a half years later he would be on this same ship again, heading toward the Klondike. He went back home with new insights into life, including the realization that he no longer wanted to "sell his muscle." He would become "a brain merchant" instead.[14] Jack London would go back to school.

"... Like a Dry Sponge"

"**A**nd no brother of mine is going to take any chewing tobacco into High School in *my* town," Eliza announced, disapproving of the bad habit her brother had learned on his trip.[1] London defended himself: He chewed tobacco to stop his teeth from aching. As further proof, he opened his mouth, revealing some empty spaces where several teeth had been pulled and the remaining teeth had decayed. Eliza made a bargain with Jack: If he would stop chewing tobacco, she would buy him a set of upper teeth and have the rest of his teeth fixed. He agreed. Eliza also presented Jack with a gift—a bicycle. One day as he coasted downhill, the force of a violent sneeze ejected his false plate and Jack, the bike, and the teeth tumbled to the ground.[2]

Each day London bicycled the forty blocks from his parents' home to Oakland High School. He quietly sat in its classrooms but felt he did not fit in. He was nineteen and older than the others. His reading and travel experiences had been so different from theirs. Many of his classmates kept their distance because of his appearance. He wore wrinkled shirts and long, baggy trousers, clothes that many of his classmates identified with the dress of street hoodlums. They saw Jack's nervousness and shyness as antisocial. Their unfriendliness toward him hurt. One of his classmates claimed London "wanted deep down in his being to be one with the class but he just couldn't."[3]

London did make some connections at school. He wrote stories for *The High School Aegis*, the school literary magazine. His two-part story on the Bonin Islands appeared on January 18 and February 1, 1895. In another piece, he wrote about the Frisco Kid, a teen tramp he had spent some time with. *The Aegis* published seven more of his articles and short stories, including "Optimism, Pessimism and Patriotism," which had a closing sentence that really upset his high school principal: "Arise, ye, Americans, patriots, and optimists! Awake! Seize the reins of a corrupted government and educate your masses."[4] As a member of the Henry Clay Club, London had the opportunity to express some of his "radical" opinions and debate important issues of the day. He liked a good argument, and in that club he seemed self-assured and confident.

His time at Oakland High School was used much differently from any of the other students'. He also worked as a janitor, sweeping the classrooms and

At Oakland High School, nineteen-year-old Jack London was older than the other students and had more experience in the world.

washing every window of the several-storied, block-long building. Every day, for two terms, he hoisted the American flag to the top of the high school building.

Whenever he had the chance, he still spent time at the Oakland Public Library surrounded by books. He read Robert Browning, Rudyard Kipling, and Robert Louis Stevenson. He met librarian Frederick Irons Bamford, who listened enthusiastically to him and suggested books to read. He also met Fred Jacobs, a student and library worker, who helped London with schoolwork and introduced him to Edward (Ted) Applegarth.

The Applegarths, an English family living in Oakland, welcomed London into their attractive home. They enjoyed his company during family dinners, picnics, literary discussions, and games of chess. London fell in love with Ted's sister, Mabel, who was three years older than he. He liked Mabel's golden hair and pretty blue eyes and attractive, long flowing skirts, but he also admired her grace, charm, education, and her love of literary classics. He melted when she recited poetry. She coached him on his grammar, encouraged more refined manners, and exchanged many letters with him. They would remain friends for life.

After just one year, London quit high school. Eliza lent him the money to attend Anderson's University Academy in Alameda, a school that prepared students to pass the entrance exams for the University of California. It was not uncommon in those days to get into a college without a high school diploma if you passed some examinations. In these "cramming schools," professors wanted their students to learn as

London, top left, enjoys a day at Yosemite State Park with the Applegarths and other friends.

fast as they could. London liked this attitude and worked feverishly. Soon Mr. Anderson, one of the administrators, called him into the office. Even though London's program of cramming two years of work into four months had been approved, Anderson now feared that the school might lose its accreditation if it allowed Jack London to do too much in such a short time. The academy dismissed London in April 1896, but gave him a full refund.[5]

Discouraged but not defeated, he crammed for the university examinations on his own. For twelve weeks he studied nineteen hours a day. Mabel Applegarth helped him in English. Fred Jacobs assisted in chemistry and physics. Bessie Maddern, Fred's fiancée, tutored Jack in advanced math. He used sample exams as study guides.

The three-day exam at the Berkeley campus began on August 10, 1896. The actual tests proved to be a lot harder than the sample tests: The university had raised its standards, without warning. Still, London passed. Now he could be admitted to the University of California at Berkeley. Johnny Heinold, owner of the First and Last Chance Saloon on the Oakland waterfront, helped him with the tuition money.

Within weeks Jack London began studies at the university. He wanted to take a dozen courses instead of the five allowed. But as the courses progressed, he felt they seemed ordinary and unexciting, rather than the challenge he expected. His professors' lack of passion about the burning issues of society embittered him.[6]

University life disillusioned him, but London realized a college diploma was important for success in society. He wanted to return for another semester but did not have the money to finish at Berkeley. He officially left on February 4, 1897, at the age of twenty-one.

Jack London may have had to abandon university life, but he did not abandon books or learning. A friend of his, novelist and short-story writer Jimmy Hopper, said Jack's brain was "like a dry sponge— impossible of saturation in its many folds."[7]

During his university days, London had been active in the Socialist Labor Party. Avidly, he read the works of Karl Marx, Herbert Spencer, and other Socialist thinkers. Several days after leaving the university, London attended a weekly meeting of the Socialist Labor Party. There some members questioned an Oakland city ordinance that stated it was unlawful for anyone to take part in a public meeting without the mayor's permission. Some of the Socialist leaders felt the law violated their rights of free speech and public assembly. London agreed and volunteered to challenge that ruling.

On February 10, 1897, London appeared in public on the steps of Oakland City Hall. He was nervous and shy, and the passion he felt did not come through in his soft voice. Yet he had challenged the law by speaking in public without the mayor's permission. He was promptly arrested. He demanded a jury trial and defended himself. Only one juror held for conviction. By the end of the month the city had dropped the case.

London's family still had financial troubles, and he thought he could help by launching his writing career.[8] He wrote essays, short stories, and poetry.

Sometimes he would be so busy, he would forget to eat. He worked on a borrowed typewriter that typed only capital letters. "The keys of that machine had to be hit so hard that to one outside the house it sounded like distant thunder or someone breaking up the furniture. . . . I strained my first fingers to the elbows, while the ends of my fingers were blisters burst and blistered again. Had it been my machine I'd have operated it with a carpenter's hammer," he remembered.[9]

Everything London had learned in the past two years went into his writing. He sold his schoolbooks to buy paper and postage stamps. He sent his work across the United States, but no one bought it. After several weeks, he packed away his notes and manuscripts. He concluded success would not come unless he studied more and practiced more.

His sister Eliza again came to his rescue. She helped get him a job at the Belmont Academy Laundry on a peninsula south of San Francisco. He would earn $30 a month, have free room and board, and still have time to learn the craft of writing. At the laundry, he sorted, washed, starched, and ironed clothing for academy students and professors and their wives.

But once again he had to do the work of two men for the pay of one. He was so tired he often fell asleep with a pen in his hand. The trunkful of books he had brought to Belmont with him remained unread. The picture was bleak.

When the academy closed for the summer, Jack London went back to Oakland. Soon he came down with a fever that swept the nation that summer of 1897—Klondike fever!

The Klondike

On July 25, 1897, Jack London and his brother-in-law, Captain James Shepard, sailed on the *Umatilla* from San Francisco. Soon they would be among 250,000 gold seekers in the Klondike River region of the Canadian Yukon. No one knew then that only about one thousand of these adventurers would return richer than when they started.

Eliza Shepard mortgaged her house to grubstake London and her husband. The two men spent $500 for a year's supply of food and equipment. Flannel shirts, extrawarm underwear, fur caps, fur-lined coats, high boots, blankets, coffee, salt meat, mining tools, and tents loaded them down. Jack London added to the heavy load with reading material, including Miner Bruce's *Alaska*. This book proved invaluable, for it told him some of what he might expect in the challenging Klondike region.

London and Shepard joined forces with three other men who had also caught Klondike fever: Merritt Sloper, Big Jim Goodman, and Fred Thompson. Their journey would not be easy.

They arrived in Juneau, Alaska, on August 2, and five days later on Dyea Beach. Confusion reigned amid the thousands of fortune hunters in Dyea. Tempers flared, shouts filled the air, supplies got mixed up, and everyone seemed to get in everyone else's way. London and his partners rushed to get on the trail. Even though it was only early August, they knew winter came early to the Klondike, and ice would soon block the rivers.

The next phase of their journey took them approximately fourteen miles to the Chilkoot Pass, described by one veteran traveler as "the worst trail this side of hell."[1] The Chilkoot Pass led straight up. It was a nightmare for travelers.

Some had money to pay the experienced Indian guides to carry the hundreds of supplies; twenty-one-year-old Jack London did not. Instead, he padded his shoulders and placed the seventy-five to one-hundred-pound loads on his back for a two-mile distance. After depositing the supplies, he returned to get another hundred pounds and patiently walked the two miles back. He made many trips, sometimes covering more than eighteen miles in one day. Even with London's help, Captain Shepard realized he could not endure the strenuous journey. He headed home.

Cold temperatures and muddy ground greeted them. Wood was scarce, so few fires were started, and there were no poles to build tents, though at times, overhanging glaciers protected the travelers. They slept very little. London and his companions remained tough and conquered this important part of the trail, but their journey was far from over.

By September 8, they set up camp at Lake Lindeman (which the Klondikers called Lake Linderman) and prepared for a difficult journey by boat on unpredictable waters. For two weeks, the men sawed spruce tree trunks into lumber and constructed the *Yukon Belle*, a twenty-seven-foot boat. They traveled miles of lakes, rapids, box canyons, and rivers. London's skill and experiences as a sailor proved invaluable. As the water rushed through narrow passageways, gaining tremendous speed, London and crew literally flew through the roaring, foaming water. They covered one mile in two minutes, miraculously avoiding the jagged riverbanks. Others were not as skilled or fortunate. The raging water capsized many boats and drowned many gold seekers.

An icy north wind and snow-covered land awaited them at Lake Laberge. Thin ice formed on the lake. If the lake froze, they would be stranded. On September 28, 1897, two months after leaving home, London announced, "Today we go through or spend the winter here with the rest. We will turn back for nothing."[2] They traveled throughout the night and reached the Thirtymile River.

By October 9, they were eighty miles from Dawson City. London and his companions made camp in an old, abandoned cabin on Split-Up Island, also called Upper Island, one of the many near the west bank of the Yukon, just below the mouth of the Stewart River. They had set their sights on Dawson City, but word spread that Dawson was overcrowded, faced a food shortage, and had no claims left to stake. London analyzed the evidence and decided to head toward Henderson Creek—the only unstaked area left in the Yukon Territory.

Gold was their goal, and they wasted little time. Big Jim Goodman, who had scouted the area, presented evidence of small golden grains. London, Goodman, and a few others set out for Henderson Creek. They spent three days prospecting. They thawed the frozen gravel with spruce fires, panned for gold, and hoped to find occasional grains of the glittering metal amid the black dirt. They found no large golden nuggets, but more of the small grains. They staked eight claims. London and friends boarded the *Yukon Belle* and drifted down to Dawson to record this claim.

Several weeks later, on November 5, 1897, Jack London solemnly swore before the gold commissioners in Dawson that he had "discovered therein a deposit of gold."[3] What London and other gold seekers did not realize at the time was that only professional mining companies with sophisticated ore-extracting machines would be able to extract large quantities of the precious gold. London and others struggled very hard that year in the Klondike, but they would never reap the huge benefits the big companies would in years to come. Jack's deposit of gold was worth only $4.50.

But London would later reap other benefits from his Klondike experience. In Dawson City he met Marshall and Louis Bond, who had been students at the prestigious Yale University in Connecticut. Their father was a well-respected judge in Santa Clara, California. London also met their dog, Jack, a cross-bred St. Bernard and Scotch shepherd (collie). The two "Jacks" became attached, and Jack the dog would eventually become the model for the famous Buck in London's *The Call of the Wild*.

Jack London, with cap pulled low on his forehead and sporting a thick, stubby beard, enjoyed discussions at the Bond cabin. Marshall Bond remembered, "Intellectually he was incomparably the most alert man in the room, and we felt it. . . . Here was a man whose life and thoughts were his own. He was refreshing."[4]

In the Klondike, the winter of 1897–1898 was long, cold, quiet, and dark. Jack London spent much of it on Split-Up Island. He later described the setting in his story "A Day's Lodging": "Ahead of him the river split into many channels to accommodate the freight of islands it carried on its breast. These islands were silent and white. No animals nor humming insects broke the silence. No birds flew in the chill air. . . . The world slept, and it was like the sleep of death."[5]

Small ten-by-twelve-foot cabins housed three or four men. Life in these close quarters was not always easy, and it was not uncommon for men to get on one another's nerves. To avoid tension with his original partners, Jack London moved into a nearby cabin with B. F. "Doc" Harvey. Inside the small cabins, ice formed on the greased-paper windows and wooden walls. Food kept on lower shelves near the floor stayed frozen. Klondikers shoveled out ice as it accumulated on the floor. Later London referred to his cabin time as "forty days in a refrigerator."[6]

His feet encased in thick woolen socks and moccasins, London passed many hours reading books, including Charles Darwin's *On the Origin of Species*, John Milton's *Paradise Lost*, Herbert Spencer's *The Philosophy of Style*, and Karl Marx's *Das Kapital*. Although he was not then writing stories, articles, or novels, the twenty-two-year-old London must have daydreamed about his career because he wrote the following on a log, high on the back wall of a cabin he stayed in for part of the winter in Henderson Creek near Split-Up Island: "Jack London miner, author Jan 27 1898."[7] He may not have realized it then, but his Klondike experience would help him write twelve books and fifty short stories.

He listened to or engaged in conversations on topics ranging from boyhood experiences to religion to social injustice. He loved hearing the adventures, part fact, part fiction, of the people who made great sacrifices to change their fortune.

Many of the men on the trail remember Jack London's acts of kindness. He shared his books, and he searched other cabins for new books to read. He did more than his share of chopping wood and offered food to anyone entering the cabin. He hiked for two days to get his buddies a plug of tobacco. One time when a man needed an operation and there was no anesthetic to give him, London freely gave the one quart of whiskey that he had packed away for such an emergency.

W. B. Hargrave, a man who befriended London in the Klondike, remembered him as an individual "who possessed the qualities of heart and mind that made him one of the world's geniuses."[8] One night they stood in awe of the aurora borealis (northern lights) in sixty-degree-below-zero weather.

In the frigid weather of the Klondike, vegetables and fruits were scarce. Most meals consisted of sourdough bread, doughnuts, beans, and bacon grease. A steady diet of these foods and lack of exercise soon took its toll on London. By May, London, like many others in the Klondike, developed scurvy, the disease caused by a lack of vitamin C. His gums swelled and bled. His teeth rattled. The few good teeth that he had left were loose. His face puffed up. If he poked a finger into his cheek, the dent remained for hours. There was no cure for scurvy in the camp. He had to leave or die.

Early in May the spring thaw opened the Yukon River. Huge cakes of ice sped by. The ice smashed into banks. It uprooted trees. Chunks of earth lifted up. As the ice jammed, the waters rose. London and his friend Doc Harvey floated down the Yukon to Dawson City on a raft made from their torn-down cabin. In Dawson they sold the logs from the raft for $600. Jack needed money for medicine. Dawson had no piped water, no sewers, and a lot of mud. It was

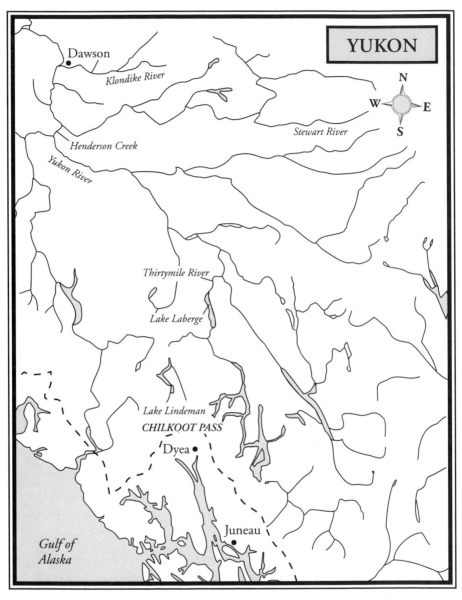

Seeking a fortune in gold, London was one of thousands who journeyed to the Klondike River region of the Canadian Yukon.

overcrowded with mosquitoes, dogs, and gold seekers. London spent most of his days at the end of May and early June with other scurvy patients in Dawson at St. Mary's Hospital run by Father William Judge, a Jesuit missionary.

Although his health improved a little, London took Father Judge's advice and headed home. Two other men joined him. London had not kept a journal of his Klondike adventures. Now, on June 8, 1898, he began a journal of his two-thousand-mile trip downriver to the mouth of the Yukon River and the sea. His body had been ravaged by disease, but his eye for detail was strong.

On Friday, June 17, he penciled the following into his diary for future use in a nature sketch for *Outing Magazine* and *Youth's Companion*: "Whole islands swept clear of trees. . . . Geese have long since disappeared, but ducks becoming quite thick as we near the mouth . . . Indian camps: fresh bear skins hanging in the sun."[9] His vision of the Klondike would soon fill thousands of pages, and he would advise writers: "Keep a notebook. Travel with it, sleep with it. Slap into it every stray thought that flutters up into your brain. Cheap paper is less perishable than gray matter, and lead pencil marking endures longer than memory."[10]

On this three-week journey in a leaky boat whose bow was a woodshed, mosquitoes swarmed over the passengers, even biting through overalls and heavy underwear.[11] London and his companions lived on salmon, wild geese, and duck. London's scurvy returned. Through the kindness of a stranger, he received raw potatoes and a can of tomatoes. In his condition these items were more valuable than gold and helped him recover from his scurvy, which at that point had almost crippled him from his waist down.

Jack London had experienced hard times in the Klondike, only to return to hard times in Oakland. Gold did not line his pockets. But golden ideas filled his mind.

6

Learning the Craft

Upon his return from the Klondike, Jack London heard the painful news that his father had died the previous fall. John London had not acquired wealth in his lifetime and had no fortune to leave his son. But before his death, he had requested that his mackintosh be left to Jack. Jack treasured that raincoat.

During the summer of 1898, work was hard to find. London's mother and his young nephew Johnny Miller needed his financial help. He trekked to employment offices and answered ads in newspapers to find work. He was unsuccessful in getting a job, and his heart had another goal: Jack London wanted to make his living by writing.

In an article of four thousand words entitled

"From Dawson to the Sea," he captured his recent twenty-five-hundred-mile exodus from the Klondike. When he queried the editor of the *San Francisco Bulletin* with his idea, he received the following response: "Interest in Alaska has subsided in an amazing degree. Then again so much has been written that I do not think it would pay us to buy your story."[1]

That fall London took the exam to qualify for the job of mail carrier at the Oakland post office. While he awaited the results, he did not earn any money except from a few occasional odd jobs. He was disheartened about his string of failures but determined to make his living as a writer. He composed poetry, short stories, essays, jokes, and sonnets. He mailed manuscript after manuscript, the return postage tucked inside. He ran out of paper and stamps. Rejection slips piled up in his small room. His bicycle, his father's mackintosh, his dress suit, his silver watch, and even his typewriter spent time in and out of the pawnshop.

In December, London received two interesting envelopes. One contained a thin letter from the *Overland Monthly* magazine, promising him only $5 for his short story "To the Man on Trail." The second contained an acceptance from *Black Cat* magazine for a science fiction story. He hoped they would pay much more than $5.

On January 16, 1899, London learned that his test score of 85.38 on the postal exam assured him a top spot on the list for mail carrier. The promise of a stable career and a comfortable salary of $65 a month, a good amount in the late 1800s, could help him and ease his mother's burden, too. But London chose to follow his mother's current advice: Pass up this security and pursue a writing career.

His $5 story, "To the Man on Trail," appeared in the *Overland Monthly*. Readers especially liked his central character, the Malemute Kid, who "lived on rabbit-tracks and salmon belly," and the Kid's toast as he glanced at frost, three inches thick inside the greased-paper window: "A health to the man on trail this night; may his grub hold out; may his dogs keep their legs; may his matches never miss fire."[2] The next issue contained London's highly praised story "The White Silence," also featuring the Malemute Kid. James Howard Bridge, the editor of the *Overland Monthly*, asked him for six more stories at $7.50 apiece and promised to feature them in the magazine. Jack London knew success would come soon.[3]

When a $40 check arrived for his story "A Thousand Deaths" in February, he finally could pay some of his debts and get some items out of the pawnshop. London wrote: "Literally and literarily, I was saved by the *Black Cat* short story."[4]

He struggled on. He kept track of every manuscript. He knew where he sent each one, how many times it had been rejected, and if it sold, how much it earned. He retired a manuscript only after forty rejections, but even then, he filed it away for future consideration.

In 1899, London mailed out 287 manuscripts. He received 266 rejection slips. His Klondike article "From Dawson to the Sea," which only a few months earlier had been rejected by the *San Francisco Examiner*, appeared in an edition of *The Illustrated Buffalo Express*.

Black Cat magazine published London's science fiction story "A Thousand Deaths" in 1899. Selling this story, said London, saved his life as a writer.

That year brought other successes as well. The *Atlantic Monthly*, a well-respected magazine that published quality literature, sent London a $120 check for his story "An Odyssey of the North." It was the largest amount he had received up to that time for his literary work. He stared lovingly at the check for a while. Then he went out and purchased a new typewriter and paid his long-overdue rent and mounting bills at the butcher shop and grocery store. When the editors suggested cutting out three thousand of his approximately twelve thousand words, he did what they asked. This edited story soon attracted the attention of East Coast book publishers, and London looked hopefully to the future.

Jack London met Cloudesley Johns, the postmaster who had written London a fan letter after reading "To the Man on Trail" and "The White Silence" in the January and February editions of the *Overland Monthly*. London responded with an encouraging letter. He and Johns, also a struggling writer, became friends. They discussed philosophy, critiqued each other's stories, and shared ways to promote their writing.

In 1899 London also met Anna Strunsky at a Socialist lecture in San Francisco. She became a powerful influence in his life, and they collaborated on *The Kempton-Wace Letters*, a fictional correspondence about the nature of love between two characters named Dane Kempton (Anna Strunsky) and Herbert Wace (Jack London).

Despite the fact that London had met with some success, he knew he had to grow as a writer and worked hard to learn the craft.[5] London believed careful reading made better writers. He continued to read Herbert Spencer, Charles Darwin, and Karl Marx. He read the scholars and philosophers Friedrich Nietzsche, Immanuel Kant, John Hobbes, John Locke, and David Hume. He read the Bible. He read William Shakespeare and Robert Louis Stevenson.

London especially admired author Rudyard Kipling, the most highly paid short-story writer of that time. He studied Kipling's work and copied his stories word for word, trying to feel his style. He said of Kipling, "I would never possibly have written anywhere near the way I did had Kipling never been."[6] He used this method to emulate other authors as well.

On small pieces of paper London wrote down words from books he read and speeches he heard—words like *palimpsest*, *badinage*, and *wizened*. He fastened them to his mirror, and he hung them on the wall and on a clothesline that zigzagged across his tiny room. He practiced them when he shaved, dressed, or combed his thick brown hair. He carried new lists in his pocket to practice when a few spare moments appeared. He used the new words, and if he used them incorrectly, he welcomed correction. He worked these new words into his writing. Sometimes they seemed forced and unnatural, but other times they were skillfully selected.

Poetry appealed to him, but he did not reveal a special talent as a poet. He continued to read and save copies of poems he discovered in magazines, feeling that a study of poetry made his prose clearer and more to the point.[7]

London wrote morning, noon, and night, but

eventually realized that he had the energy to write effectively for only a part of each day. He established this routine: Begin early in the morning and write one thousand words a day. When he fell behind, he wrote more the next day. He limited his sleep to five and a half hours a night. As London said of his autobiographical character Martin Eden: "He hated the oblivion of sleep. There was too much to do, too much of life to live."[8]

Part of living for Jack London included flying colorful kites, sometimes six at a time, swimming, sailing, boxing, fencing, debating, and bike riding. He said riding a bike was "something that makes life worth living."[9]

At times he rode his bike with his dear friend and former math tutor, Bessie Maddern. She had been engaged to their mutual friend Fred Jacobs, who died of a tropical fever on his way to fight in the Spanish-American War of 1898. Bessie and Jack liked going on picnics, developing photographs, and reviewing Jack's manuscripts. One day, without a lot of thought, London suddenly proposed marriage to her. "We have such fun together," he reminded her.[10] He was honest and told her that he did not love her. She was sure they would fall in love. The following Saturday, April 7, 1900, they were married in a very simple ceremony.

On their wedding day, *The Son of the Wolf*—London's collection of Yukon stories, including "To the Man on Trail"—was published. Many critics wrote favorable reviews, and it became one of the publisher's top sellers in 1900.

Soon London was hailed an "American Kipling."[11] Now magazines wanted Jack London's work. They accepted many of his stories that had previously been rejected. In the twentieth century his lively action stories proved popular. More people were reading, and book and magazine sales soared. London still sent out manuscripts and still received rejections, but in 1900 he earned $2,534.13 from writing, a sizable sum in those days,

A New York book publisher, S. S. McClure, gave London $100 per month to write a novel. This deal took some of the financial pressure from him, but there was a new price to pay: Even before he completed *A Daughter of the Snows*, he was disappointed in the book. Despite his frustration, he saw the project through. He wrote to his friend Cloudesley Johns:

Dear Cloudesley:

Well, I am on the home stretch of the novel, and it is a failure. This is not said in a fit of the blues, but from calm conviction. However, on the other hand, I have learned a great deal concerning the writing of novels. On this one which I have attempted, I could write three books of equal size showing wherein I failed, and why, and laying down principles violated, etc. O, it's been a great study. I shall be at work finishing it for the rest of the month—you know I always finish whatever I begin. I never leave a thing in such a state that in the time to come haunting thoughts creep in—"If I had only gone on, etc."[12]

McClure refused to publish *A Daughter of the Snows*, but J. B. Lippincott in Philadelphia published it instead. Many reviewers criticized London for his poor portrayal of his female character Frona Welse, who had braved life in the Klondike. A few reviewers, however, did believe London was ahead of his time in portraying an independent woman. London scholar Franklin Walker later commented: "The trouble was that he tried to write a romance with little knowledge of pace, sustained character development or social comedy. It was not his kind of book."[13]

In the first month of 1901, on January 15, the Londons' first daughter was born. Bessie selected the name Joan from a list in her husband's file containing names he admired for women. Virginia Prentiss (Mammy Jennie), who had taken care of Jack when he was a baby, moved in to help take care of little Joan London.

During 1901, London began writing feature articles for the *San Francisco Examiner*. He also ran unsuccessfully for mayor of Oakland. He lectured on topics of war, women's suffrage (the right to vote), and the tramp, and published his second collection of stories set in the Klondike, *The God of His Fathers*.

In the final months of 1901, George P. Brett, president of the prestigious Macmillan Publishing Company in New York, asked London for material. London soon received a contract from Macmillan for *The Children of the Frost*, a collection of ten Klondike stories told from the Indians' point of view.

The Londons rented an attractive bungalow in the Oakland hills, amid pines and eucalyptus trees and fields of tall grasses and orange poppies. When the fog lifted, they had a beautiful view of San Francisco Bay.

After a morning of writing, Jack London especially enjoyed his Wednesday afternoons and evenings when his friends would join him for card games, singing, poetry readings, kite flying, and fencing. Although he liked the role of "generous host," his wife, Bessie, was often uncomfortable with these weekly gatherings filled with food, drink, humor, and practical jokes.[14] She grew to resent them and the added expense on their budget. And Jack London was often in debt. He supported his mother and nephew, and he helped old friends. He would lend money, even though he realized he would never be repaid.

On July 21, 1902, London was $3,000 in debt and Bessie was pregnant with their second child. He was relieved when the American Press Association in New York offered him an assignment in South Africa.[15] The Boer War had just ended, and the association wanted London to interview famous officers to discuss the postwar situation in South Africa. The trip was canceled suddenly when the Press Association learned that the officers to be interviewed had left Capetown for Europe. Jack London came up with a new idea. He wanted to go to London, England, and write about the East End slums.

In August, twenty-six-year-old Jack London arrived in England alone and took on a new identity: that of a stranded American sailor who had lost his money and clothes. He lived in the East End, where he made these observations:

> *The color of life is gray and drab. Everything is helpless, hopeless, unrelieved, and dirty. Bathtubs are a*

thing totally unknown, as mythical as the ambrosia of the gods. . . . Strange vagrant odors come drifting along the greasy wind, and the rain, when it falls, is more like grease than water from heaven. . . . A new race had sprung up, a street people. They pass their lives at work and in the streets.[16]

London learned that the majority of people were there, not by choice or laziness, but because of old age, disease, or accident. He stood with them in breadlines, joined them in the workhouse and in their desperate search for jobs that paid very little. He witnessed how the authorities kept them on the run during the night, forbidding them to sleep in the park or on benches.

During his eighty-six days in the East End, London also read books, examined thousands of pamphlets, newspapers, and magazines, and took photographs for his book titled *The People of the Abyss* (author H. G. Wells's term for the urban poor).[17] In it, he urged readers to consider the suffering of others:

Where you would not have your own babe live, and develop, and gather to itself knowledge of life and the things of life, is not a fit place for the babes of other men to live and develop, and gather to themselves knowledge of life and the things of life. . . . What is not good enough for you is not good enough for other men and there is no more to be said.[18]

The sight of hungry people picking through garbage for food or wrapping their feet in filthy rags haunted Jack. He hated that punishments were harsher for people convicted of stealing food when

In 1902, to do research for his book The People of the Abyss, London spent about three months living with the poor in the slums of England's East End.

they were hungry than they were for people convicted of assaulting a human being.

On August 21, 1902, he wrote to Anna Strunsky: "I find it almost impossible to believe that some of the horrible things I have seen are really so."[19] The next day he wrote to his friends George and Caroline Sterling: "I think I should die if I had to live two years in the East End of London."[20]

Jack London was well aware of his good fortune of being able to escape the life in the East End of London while other inhabitants were condemned to die there. When his project was complete, he toured France, Germany, and Italy. Tucked inside his suitcase was the complete manuscript of *The People of the Abyss*, which would be published the following year by Macmillan.

Upon arriving in New York City on November 4, 1902, London borrowed $150 from George P. Brett to get home. He was eager to see his new baby daughter, born on October 20 while he was in Europe. She was named Bess but would later be called Becky.

By the time London arrived in California, thousands of American bookshelves contained copies of his newly published books: *A Daughter of the Snows*, *The Children of the Frost*, and *The Cruise of the Dazzler*.

London would soon write more books to fill those shelves. On December 1, 1902, he feverishly began writing *The Call of the Wild*. He wrote to Anna Strunsky: "It started as a companion to my other dog story, 'Batard' which you may remember, but it got away from me and instead of 4,000 words it ran 32,000 before I could call a halt."[21] ("Batard," originally titled "Diable: A Dog," portrayed the dog as a vicious beast.)

The Call of the Wild tells the tale of a dog named Buck who is stolen from his comfortable home in California and adapts to become an excellent sled dog. London's philosophy shines through: his admiration for the fighter, his sympathy for the underdog, and his belief that those who adapt to change are the ones who survive.

Although London had an excellent memory for detail, recalling the sights, sounds, smells, tastes, and feelings of his own Klondike experience, he also recognized the importance of research. He talked to other Klondike survivors and read books and old newspaper articles about the gold rush. During the same year he began writing *The Call of the Wild*, a book entitled *My Dogs in the Northland* by Egerton R. Young appeared on the scene. In Young's nonfiction book, London discovered that sled dogs dug places deep in the snow to use as beds and shamelessly stole another dog's spot when that dog was away. He learned that Young's dogs howled at the nighttime hours of nine, twelve, and three. He also learned that when sled dogs felt pain in their paws, they held them up to be protected with hide or leather. Young's firsthand experiences with sled dogs helped London create fascinating scenes such as this in *The Call of the Wild*:

> *Buck's feet were not so compact and hard as the feet of the huskies. His had softened during the many generations since the day his last wild ancestor was tamed by a cave-dweller or river man. All day long he limped in agony, and camp once made, lay down like a dead dog. Hungry as he was, he would not move to receive his ration of fish, which Francois had*

to bring to him. Also, the dog driver rubbed Buck's feet for half an hour each night after supper, and sacrificed the tops of his own moccasins for Buck. This was a great relief, and Buck caused even the weazened face of Perrault to twist itself into a grin one morning, when Francois forgot the moccasins and Buck lay on his back, his four feet waving appealing in the air, and refused to budge without them. Later his feet grew hard to the trail, and the worn-out foot-gear was thrown away.[22]

On January 26, 1903, less than two months after he had begun *The Call of the Wild*, London first sent the manuscript to the *Saturday Evening Post*. The magazine agreed to publish it for $750 if he cut out five thousand words. He accepted. It was serialized from June 20 to July 18, 1903. Next, Macmillan Publishing Company bought the book rights for a flat fee of $2,000. Even though *The Call of the Wild* would have made him at least a million dollars in book royalties during his lifetime, Jack London never regretted his decision to accept the flat fee. He was happy with the way Macmillan promoted him as a writer.[23]

In the summer of 1903, the fifth year after London's return from the Klondike, *The Call of the Wild* became a sensation. It sold out its entire first edition of ten thousand copies within twenty-four hours. Many found it difficult to put down the rich green leather-covered edition featuring the title and author in striking gold letters. Jack London had succeeded in writing a best-seller.

Jack and Charmian

At the age of twenty-seven, Jack
London achieved recognition as a writer, but his
marriage was an unhappy one. He and Bessie were
good friends when they married, but he had been
honest and told her that he did not love her. During
their three-year marriage, even their friendship faded.
He was falling in love with the fun-loving, adventurous
Charmian Kittredge, whom he had met in 1900 when
her aunt Mrs. Ninetta Eames was writing a magazine
article about him. In July 1903, London told Bessie
he was leaving her.

Using some of his earnings from *The Call of the
Wild*, London purchased a single-masted sailboat
named the *Spray*. Sailing on the breathtaking San

Francisco Bay and some of the nearby rivers that emptied into it helped him get in touch with his beloved water again. He continued to write *The Sea Wolf*, a novel drawn from his experiences aboard the *Sophia Sutherland* and from sea stories he had heard.

On January 7, 1904, London was sent by ship to Yokohama and Korea. Japan and Russia would soon be at war. He was one of seven correspondents representing press associations and great newspapers of the world with the first Japanese Army Corps. He wrote home in March: "Just caught five body lice on my undershirt. . . . Lice drive me clean crazy. I am itching all over. I am sure every second, that a score of them are on me."[1]

The Japanese did not believe a war correspondent

Japanese soldiers during the Russo-Japanese War in 1904. London was sent to Japan as a newspaper correspondent.

was valuable.[2] It frustrated London that correspondents had to keep to the rear of the firing lines and were forbidden to "explore" on their own: "The nearest I have succeeded in getting to a Japanese battery [a military unit], and one not in action either, was when I crawled to the top of a hill half a mile to the rear and gazed upon it through field glasses in fear and trembling."[3]

Although he admitted, "I've wasted five months of my life in this war,"[4] readers gained new insights from his articles in the *San Francisco Examiner*, especially the one dated Sunday, June 5, 1904, in which he showed how warfare of ancient times compared with that of modern days.[5]

Upon his return, Jack London faced a bitter divorce suit from Bessie. The divorce was granted on November 11, 1904, under the condition that Jack must wait one year to remarry. He continued to support Bessie and his two daughters for the rest of his life.

While London was in Korea, he had authorized George Sterling and Charmian to help edit *The Sea Wolf* manuscript. It was published the first week of October 1904 and rose high on the best-seller list.

The year 1905 proved to be a busy one. London began writing *White Fang*, his well-known novel about a wild wolf cub who is taken out of the Klondike and sent to California. The book is a companion story to *The Call of the Wild*, in which a California dog becomes wild. London also purchased approximately 130 acres of land in Glen Ellen, California. Over the years he would buy more land until his Beauty

Ranch, as he called it, would encompass fourteen hundred acres.

That September the *San Francisco Examiner* paid him $100 to cover the Jimmy Britt-Battling Nelson lightweight fight. He saw challenger Oscar (Battling) Nelson knock out Britt in the eighteenth round. London relished this assignment because boxing was his favorite sport. He and Charmian, a true adventurer herself, often put on gloves and sparred with each other.

In mid-October 1905 he began a nationwide lecture tour, addressing topics concerning the working class, child labor, the Klondike, and his struggle to become a writer. A powerful and passionate speaker, he frequently waved his arms and gestured with his hands. Some applauded him; others condemned him. *The New York Times* took some of London's phrases and statements out of context, inflaming many readers.[6] Critics labeled Jack London anti-American and criticized him for preaching violence, but he viewed these lectures as an attempt to enlighten the rich to become aware of the plight of the poor.

On November 18, 1905, while lecturing in Ohio, Jack received word that his divorce from Bessie was final. Jack wired Charmian, and the next day they were married by a notary public in a simple ceremony. Not everyone reacted well. Society did not accept divorce, and some saw London as abandoning his wife and two daughters, which he had not.[7]

This second marriage and his socialist beliefs caused a backlash against London. Some scheduled lectures were canceled; some libraries refused to put

Jack London with daughters Becky, left, and Joan, right, in 1905.

his work on the shelf; and some people refused to read his books. A cry was issued: "Boycott all magazines which contain stories by Jack London."[8]

Jack and Charmian did not care. They loved each other deeply.[9] The tour continued, this time with Charmian by his side, but two days before Christmas, they headed for Jamaica on a long-awaited honeymoon. The lecture tour resumed in early 1906.

Despite some criticism, enthusiastic letters still poured in from all over the world, including Russia, Sweden, and Australia. Fans told him they loved his stories, they shared his affection for dogs, or they, too, wanted to be writers. Many fans requested autographs. One from New Jersey wrote: "I am a young boy collecting autographs. May I have yours?"[10]

Letters were always answered and whenever possible, Jack London honored his fans' requests, including requests for money.

For the rest of her husband's life, Charmian helped Jack with his correspondence. Even though he had kept excellent records documenting where and when he sent his writing, he discarded the actual manuscripts after they were published. Charmian made sure that did not happen after they were together. Thanks to her, many of his manuscripts still exist. They are housed at the Huntington Library in San Marino, California, which has a very large collection of Jack London material.

Jack enjoyed reading his morning's work to Charmian. She loved examining his handwritten pages before she typed them. Sometimes even a friendly conversation about the family dog could spark a story idea: Jack adopted an old Klondiker's brown-and-white husky after the man died. Every chance Brown Wolf got, he escaped and returned to his dead owner's house. After Jack repeatedly sent someone to retrieve him, he was about to give up and let the dog have his way. At that moment Brown Wolf decided to stay. Jack welcomed the husky's return with open arms, and the two bonded. Charmian asked, "Now what do you suppose Brown Wolf would do if his old master should suddenly pop up beside you?"

Jack replied, half smiling, "A story right there—don't breathe another word for a minute." He quickly scribbled words onto a notepad, and soon he captivated the world with a story titled "Brown Wolf."[11]

Brown Wolf spent many a day with his new master, often lying beside him as he read on a hammock beneath the laurels. Sometimes London would plot out a novel in a nearby manzanita grove. While he wrote, he often listened to Charmian's piano playing or phonograph records.

Jack and Charmian rode all over the beautiful Sonoma Valley beneath redwoods, oaks, maples, and leather-leafed madronas. During the early years of their marriage, they lived in a cabin at Wake Robin Lodge in Glen Ellen, California. Jack taught the young campers who vacationed nearby to swim and dive, box, and wrestle.

Charmian loved horses and Jack had learned to saddle and harness them. He remembered the horrible conditions horses had endured in the Klondike, and he treated his very well. He often rode on Washoe-Ban, a chestnut-gold thoroughbred. One night Washoe-Ban's leg became entangled in a piece of barbed wire. There was no hope for the horse, whose hind leg had been sawed nearly through by the wire. The next day Jack and Charmian cried in each other's arms as the shot rang out from the ranch foreman's gun, putting their beloved horse out of his misery.

Plans for a seven-year cruise around the world fascinated both of them. On a large globe they purchased for their future library, they traced their anticipated route—Hawaii, the South Seas, Samoa, Tasmania, New Zealand, Australia, New Guinea, the Philippines, Japan, Korea, China, India, the Red Sea, the Mediterranean Sea, the Black Sea, the Baltic Sea, across the Atlantic to New York, around the Horn, and

London enjoyed the companionship of his adopted brown-and-white husky, Brown Wolf.

back to San Francisco. Jack's affectionate nickname for Charmian was Mate-Woman, and as part of an inscription in a book to her he wrote: ". . . and we shall be mates around the whole round world."[12]

Construction of their yacht began. Jack named the yacht *Snark* after Lewis Carroll's poem "The Hunting of the Snark." Carroll had created the imaginary snark by blending a snake and a shark. London believed that "boats like horses and dogs, should have names of one syllable. Good, sharp, strong names that can never be mis-heard."[13] The *Snark* measured forty-three feet on the waterline and fifty-five feet overall. It had three staterooms, an engine room, bathroom, and galley. When it entered the rivers, the masts would be lowered and the engine would take over.

Jack's motto regarding the cruise was, Spare no expense.[14] He anticipated that the *Snark* would cost between $7,000 and $10,000. Jack and Charmian enthusiastically prepared for the cruise by ordering items featured in newspapers, magazines, and catalogs. They were as happy as children on Christmas Day as they opened their morning mail filled with large and small packages including fishing tackle, neckerchiefs, and strings of beads.[15]

The San Francisco earthquake of 1906 interrupted their plans. On the morning of April 18, Jack and Charmian London saw a huge column of smoke in the direction of San Francisco. They soon heard reports of a raging fire attacking San Francisco, the result of a thirty-second quake that had twisted the city. Hours later they were there, walking hand in hand through the destruction. Jack wrote an account, titled "Story of an Eyewitness," that makes the reader aware of the human side of the disaster:

Before the flames, throughout the night, fled tens of thousands of homeless ones. Some were wrapped in blankets. Others carried bundles of bedding and dear household treasures. Sometimes a whole family was harnessed to a carriage or delivery wagon that was weighted down with their possessions. Baby buggies, toy wagons, and go-carts were used as trucks, while every other person was dragging a trunk. Yet everybody was gracious. The most perfect courtesy obtained [prevailed]. Never, in all San Francisco's history, were her people so kind and courteous as on this night of terror.[16]

Because of the earthquake, the cost of labor and materials soared for the *Snark*. It totaled $30,000. A year later, in April 1907, Charmian, Jack, and a small crew finally sailed from the San Francisco harbor into the waters of the Pacific.

Problems plagued their journey. Inferior materials had been used during construction, and the boat had been badly damaged in one of its trial runs. Four watertight compartments leaked the entire two thousand miles to Hawaii. Gasoline leaked into the tools and food supply. The captain, an experienced inland sailor, did not know how to navigate on the open sea, and the crew did not work well together. For various reasons, several crew changes were made when the *Snark* reached Hawaii. Nakata, a young man from Japan, joined the *Snark* when they left

Jack and Charmian look at the drawings for their boat—the Snark—on which they planned to cruise around the world for seven years. This was their favorite photograph taken together.

Hawaii. He would remain with the Londons years after the journey.

The five months spent in the Hawaiian Islands were productive times. Jack learned to surf as skillfully as the natives. His detailed articles about surfing helped make it a popular sport.

Jack and Charmian lived in a leper colony on Molokai for one week. Jack read every book possible, talked with doctors, and associated with those who suffered from leprosy, a disease that attacks the skin and nerves. He used his research to write "The Lepers of Molokai," published in the *Woman's Home Companion*. In it he emphasized the happiness created in that colony despite the physical suffering.

Before he left Hawaii, he finished the second version of "To Build a Fire" (nearly three times longer and featuring a very different ending from the one in the first version, written in 1901). He also had begun the novel *Martin Eden* (he started out calling it *Success*).

Their cruise was an adventurous blend of time on land and sea. Charmian described Jack's enthusiasm aboard the *Snark*:

> *Jack has a delightful characteristic of always wanting to share everything in which he is interested—his amusements, his books, or the thing he is studying. He explains to me his advancing steps in navigation; he reads aloud to me; he wants me to feel the tug of his fish on the line; and he draws all of us together to re-read aloud, some book he knows will give pleasure. Sunday forenoon, having done more than his usual "stint" of writing the previous day, he*

took a holiday and read Conrad's Typhoon *aloud to the delight of the sailormen.*[17]

After Hawaii, the Londons and crew set sail for the Marquesas Islands, two thousand miles south and a little east of Hawaii, then on to Tahiti, approximately one thousand miles to the southwest. On their journey to Tahiti, Jack and Charmian spent sixty days without seeing other ships.

Jack wrote and kept in touch with business back home through letters and coded telegrams. Not every message from home was a happy one. News of financial troubles arrived, too. In mid-January, nine months after they first set sail on the *Snark*, the Londons returned home on the S.S. *Mariposa* to straighten out business affairs. They visited Jack's daughters and got their finances in order. By February 14 they were back in the seaport of Papeete on Tahiti and soon back aboard the *Snark*.

They swam in the sunsets and savored the balmy breezes scented with tropical flowers and coconut. Charmian played her ukulele. Jack read aloud, wrote books, short stories, and articles, following his schedule of writing one thousand words a day. He shopped for special souvenirs, including dolls and jewelry for his daughters. In a letter to his younger daughter, Becky, he wrote from the Solomon Islands:

> *Tell mama that I say that the pearls and rings and all the things I send you and Joan, are for you to have and use now. Never mind waiting until you are older. . . .*
>
> *Tell Joan I am writing a novel and that I have*

named the girl in it Joan. When you are older I shall name a girl in one of my books after you. With a whole armful of love,

Daddy.[18]

When in Apia, Samoa, they visited the grave of Robert Louis Stevenson, one of London's boyhood idols.

One day on the *Snark,* a brightly colored bird dropped from the sky and landed at Charmian's feet. It was exhausted. Charmian tried to comfort it. Jack quickly got a book to research the type of bird, but the information was not to be found. He guessed the bird must be a land bird. He changed course and set the

London and his wife, Charmian, had many adventures as they circled the globe aboard the Snark.

bird free as he steered close to shore. The bird, which had regained its strength, flew into the safety of the coconut trees. One of the crew members commented: "I have little doubt that this is the only time a captain ever went twenty miles out of his way when his fuel was low (our gasoline tanks were fast emptying), just to put a poor little bird ashore to go back to its mate and its young."[19]

Adjusting to tropical climates and battling strange diseases was not easy. Jack's hands swelled, his skin flaked, and he suffered from yaws, a tropical disease that causes reddish sores on the skin. Malaria and yellow fever plagued the crew. The breakdown of Jack's health finally called an end to the cruise of the *Snark* in Sydney, Australia. Much later they sold the *Snark* to an English company for just a fraction of its original cost.

While recuperating in Sydney, Jack London was paid $275 to report on the world heavyweight boxing championship between Jack Burns and Tommy Johnson. Charmian had special permission to view the fight, and she was the only woman in the crowd of twenty thousand spectators.

In London's account of the match, he wrote:

> There was never so one-sided a world's champion-ship in the history of the ring. . . . Johnson was too big, too able, too clever, too superb. He was impreg-nable. His long arms, his height, his cool-seeing eyes, his timing and distancing, his footwork, his blocking and locking, and his splendid out-sparring and equally splendid in-fighting kept Burns in trouble all the time.[20]

As the Londons sailed back toward home on the steamer *Tymeric*, Jack listened carefully to Captain McIlwaine reminisce about his sea experiences. The recollections inspired the stories "Samuel" and "The Sea Farmer." After stops in Ecuador and the Panama Canal Zone (the canal was not used until 1914), they arrived in New Orleans, Louisiana, on the S.S. *Turriaba*.

On July 21, 1909, they were back home in Glen Ellen at Wake Robin Lodge. Soon Jack was feeling healthier. He recorded his impression of his twenty-six-month journey in *The Cruise of the Snark*. Charmian, who kept an excellent diary on this trip of the South Seas, told her story in *The Log of the Snark*.

Charmian became pregnant. Jack prayed for a son but was delighted when on June 19, 1910, another daughter was born. "Boy or girl it doesn't matter . . . as long as it's Charmian's," he said.[21] Their happiness was short-lived. The baby they named Joy died thirty-eight hours later.

8

The Final Years

After their newborn daughter's death, Jack and Charmian still had each other, and the sea seemed to bring them peace. They purchased a forty-year-old boat and had the hull and rigging overhauled. They added a little coal stove for cooking and warmth in the winter. The *Roamer* would be their vessel for many trips, lasting weeks, and sometimes months. While on board, they read, played cards, wrote, laughed, and sang. They fished for rock cod, striped bass, and sea trout. One Thanksgiving on the *Roamer*, they feasted on a dinner of geese, duck, oysters, pumpkin, and cranberries.

Jack London, who as a boy had built his Alhambra out of discarded chimney bricks, dreamed

Jack London in his famous pose on the Roamer *in 1910.*

of an Alhambra of his own on Beauty Ranch. It would be known as "Wolf House," for Jack liked to be called Wolf, a name his friend the poet George Sterling gave to him. London's Wolf House would tower four stories high and have twenty-six rooms and nine fireplaces. The dining room would hold fifty people comfortably. A spiral staircase would lead from a large library to his workroom. Charmian's Steinway grand piano and Jack's great collection of books would have places of honor.

In 1911 construction on the home began. Horse-drawn wagons carried volcanic rocks, blue slate, and huge pieces of redwood, much of it with its bark left intact, to the building site. Jack appeared often to check the progress.

He loved Beauty Ranch with its spectacular views of the surrounding valleys and mountains. Each year he made additional improvements: A bamboo grove eventually encircled their frog pond, stone winery buildings became stables, new riding trails were cleared. The ranch featured two concrete-block silos, twelve feet in diameter, the first of their kind in California.

The "piggery," invented by Jack, became known worldwide. It was a circular building made of concrete and stone with seventeen apartments for seventeen pig families, each with its individual runway, for the pigs to get to their trough. A special system for cleansing and disinfecting kept everything fresh.

After reading articles that proclaimed eucalyptus the "timber of the future," Jack had more than one hundred thousand eucalyptus trees planted on

Beauty Ranch. Their silvery bark added beauty to the ranch, but interest in the trees died down, and he never made the fortune he hoped for from investing in them.

Jack London, a self-taught writer, now became a self-taught farmer. He read every book, article, and manual he possibly could on topics ranging from alfalfa to soil erosion. He often inquired about the daily workings of the farm through notes written on small pieces of yellow paper left for his sister Eliza, whom he had hired to manage the farm, or for other workers: "Are the avocados we planted alive? Let me know."[1]

He was proud to call himself "farmer" and practiced Chinese farming methods, which rotated crops and did not use commercial fertilizers. As Jack approached his late thirties, it seemed to Charmian that he was "far more interested in introducing better farming into Sonoma County and the country at large than he was in leaving behind a masterpiece of literature."[2]

In 1911, Jack and Charmian hitched four saddle horses to a Studebaker wagon packed with a typewriter and books. Jack's valet Nakata accompanied them. They traveled fifteen hundred miles to Oregon and back to learn about the beautiful countryside that neighbored them. Although cars were available at that time, Jack preferred an old-fashioned means of transportation: "We don't mix with gasoline very well," he admitted.[3] As they arrived in small towns, Jack stopped at local saloons to buy a drink for the bartender and patrons. In return, they told him the best roads to travel and the locations of good fishing streams.

When the Londons returned from their three-month wagon ride, they moved from Wake Robin Lodge to a cottage on Beauty Ranch until the construction of Wolf House was completed. Because of their different sleeping habits, Jack and Charmian each had a separate glassed-in sleeping porch. Jack's bed was covered with a favorite coyote rug and several large pillows to support him during his long hours of reading or writing. Nakata placed plenty of sharp pencils at his bedside as well as large and small writing pads, cigarettes, and a brass ashtray from Korea.

In 1911, the Londons moved into this white-framed wood house called "The Cottage" while their luxury home, Wolf House, was being built.

Within easy reach were dishes of fruit or dried fish, and thermos bottles of beverages, usually water, grape juice, and buttermilk. Newspapers and magazines, neatly arranged according to dates, the latest on top, were stacked nearby.

Jack had his coffee at six and breakfast at seven. His mornings were devoted to writing. Even though at this stage in his life he was the best known, highest paid, and most popular writer in the world, he was finding the task exceedingly difficult. "I detest writing. On the other hand, it is the best way I have ever found to make a very good living,"[4] he explained. Jack London had always been honest in saying that he wrote for the money, not for the fame or love of it.

Each day Nakata rang a bronze gong to signal their main meal, served at 12:30. One of Jack's most requested meals each fall season was wild duck, cooked rare, accompanied by potatoes au gratin. He washed it down with imported Liebfraumilch wine sipped from a favorite tall, shimmering opaline glass.

Since his love for poetry was still strong, Jack brought out old binders filled with poetry and read from them. He collected the latest poems, including John Masefield's "The Everlasting Mercy," which he insisted on reading to everyone who visited. Charmian described his reading voice as "full of music."[5]

In between times at Beauty Ranch, there were adventures. In 1912, Jack and Charmian, Nakata, and a newly purchased fox-terrier puppy named Possum sailed on the *Dirigo*, a steel windjammer. Their journey, which would help Jack get more background material for a sea novel, took one hundred forty-eight days. They traveled from Baltimore to Seattle via Cape Horn, the most southerly part of South America. Many sailors dreaded "rounding the Horn" because of the seemingly endless storms and fog, but that was a challenge to the Londons. While they avoided disaster, another ship on the seas that year did not fare as well: The *Titanic* sank on April 15, 1912.

Jack brought the dental kit he had kept on the *Snark* and pulled teeth for the *Dirigo* crew. He also played dentist to Possum who had a hard time getting rid of his puppy molars. Jack later honored Possum by making him a character in *The Mutiny of the Elsinore*, based on their voyage around Cape Horn, as well as in the novel *Valley of the Moon*, set in the Sonoma Valley. Possum returned to the Beauty Ranch with them and became a beloved pet.

Several days after their return to the ranch, Charmian suffered a miscarriage. Their chances of having a child together faded. Charmian's miscarriage seemed like an omen for the year ahead.

The year 1913 was an extremely trying one for Jack. His nephew Irving Shepard was nearly electrocuted by accident; bad weather ruined a fruit crop; a prized mare, in foal, was found shot in a field; grasshoppers devoured the leaves of his eucalyptus trees; and he had surgery to remove his appendix. Dr. William S. Porter told Jack that his kidneys were damaged and warned him of an early death if he did not avoid raw fish, meat, and alcohol.[6] In addition to this shocking news, he also faced a legal battle regarding motion picture rights to his books.

Jack London's wife, Charmian, and their fox-terrier, Possum.

The costs for Wolf House mounted, and the figure hit close to $75,000, an enormous amount in that day. Jack knew it was expensive, but he said, "When it is done, I shall be really comfortable for the first time in my life."[7] Jack never knew that comfort.

Wolf House burned on August 22, 1913, just a few weeks before Jack and Charmian were planning to move in. At first, arson was suspected, but in later years it was concluded that spontaneous combustion had caused the fire. Internal heat had built up in oily rags left by workers during a very dry August, and the rags burst into flames.

Jack tried to hold back his emotions, knowing that his reaction could not rebuild the house. But when the senseless loss of such a beautiful building hit him, he lay in Charmian's arms and shook like a child.[8]

Life on the ranch continued, and Jack's responsibilities increased. When he reported on the Mexican Revolution for *Collier's* magazine in 1914, his articles against the revolt angered many Socialists. The rift between them deepened, and two years later he resigned from the Socialist Party, even though he still advocated social revolution.

Stress from a hectic schedule and health problems often made him irritable. He felt bitterness that his first wife, Bessie, would not let his daughters visit him at the ranch. He wanted them near him, but Bess resented Charmian and did not want the girls around her.[9] Daughter Joan was caught in the middle, and she and her father exchanged harsh letters on the topic.[10]

Hoping his health would improve, he made two

The stone-walled ruins of Wolf House can still be seen today. The library would have been large enough to house Jack London's collection of fifteen thousand books.

trips to Hawaii, each lasting five to six months, one in 1915 and the other the following year. Hawaiian trips were peaceful times. After his morning writing routine, he and Charmian read, relaxed, and visited with friends.

On October 22, 1916, one of his horses, a purebred English shire named Neuadd Hillside, died during the night. The next day Jack's face was tear-stained as he stayed close to Charmian, telling her how much that beautiful horse meant to him. Days later a package arrived in the mail containing two gold medals won by Neuadd Hillside at a recent state exhibit. Jack teared up again. "They can't forget that poor fellow even though he is dead. The prizes keep coming in."[11]

Then London had to be in court concerning a lawsuit his neighbors brought against him. They accused him of diverting an important source of water—the Graham Creek. London testified that when he bought Beauty Ranch, he purchased the main water rights to the creek, which flowed through the land. The amount he took would not deprive others of water. The court ruled in his favor.

On November 17, 1916, London hosted a luncheon for the same neighbors who had sued him. He wanted no ill will between them. He wanted them to see what the water from Graham Creek could do for agriculture. He was cordial at the party, but guests noticed that his face was "puffy," his body appeared bloated. He felt ill.

A history of kidney problems had plagued Jack London, and at that time there were no transplants or dialysis machines. His weak kidneys could not clear the toxins from his blood. The toxins made him feverish and at times very excitable, at times argumentative. One visitor noted that Jack had lost "both the old gleam in his eye and the familiar laughter."[12]

On November 21, 1916, Jack wrote a brief letter to his daughters, making plans to meet them away from Beauty Ranch. It would be the last letter he would ever write.

Glen Ellen
Nov. 21, 1916

Dear Joan:—

Next Sunday, will you and Bess have lunch with me at Saddle Rock, and, if weather is good, go for a sail with me on Lake Merrit.

If weather is not good, we can go to a matinee of some sort.
Let me know at once.
I leave Ranch next Friday.
I leave Calif. Wednesday following.

Daddy[13]

Jack London entered a coma and died at 7:45 P.M., Wednesday, November 22, 1916. He was forty years old. The unfinished manuscript of *Cherry* lay on his worktable.

The official cause of death stands as uremic poisoning due to kidney failure.

At his wake in their cottage, Jack London's body rested in a gray casket, dressed in a gray suit, the color he wore when he first met Charmian.

Jack London's grave site is visited by people from around the world.

The following day, Charmian stayed behind as Eliza accompanied Jack's body to the crematory and a short service in Oakland. She thought this was the time for his first wife and daughters and did not want to interfere.[14]

On Sunday morning, November 26, 1916, Charmian twined fern and yellow primrose from their garden around the small copper urn containing Jack's ashes. She also added a dried rust-colored Hawaiian lei as a tribute to Jack's adopted home of Hawaii. In the November rain she carried the urn to the wagon, the same wagon that in life Jack had driven with a team of four horses.

As the urn was placed into the ground and encased in concrete, rays of sun broke through the gray sky. There were no words. No prayers. As he wished, his remains were buried next to the Greenlaw children, who had been buried on the land long before he purchased it. A huge, moss-covered red boulder from the remains of Wolf House was rolled into place, as London had requested.

The next day, November 27, was Charmian's forty-fifth birthday. Six months after Jack's death, his beloved terrier, Possum, drowned in the patio pool at the remains of Wolf House. Charmian buried him close by his master "where," she said, "a true dog should lie."[15]

The London Legacy

As the world learned of Jack London's death, messages flooded in offering praise and words of comfort. One admirer wrote: "To me it seems like having a light turned off, with too few already burning, leaving the road darker and more dismal and difficult."[1]

Another reflected: "He had lived with down and outs, and with animals. . . . And he wrote their tragic lives as no human ever wrote them before."[2]

On Monday, December 4, 1916, the city of Sonoma, in the Valley of the Moon, closed its businesses from 1:00 to 1:15 P.M. to honor Jack London's memory.

Days later, movie patrons watched a newsreel of Jack London, filmed shortly before his death. They watched him admiring his horses, showing off Beauty Ranch, and cuddling piglets.

Jack London never got to write his autobiography, which he hoped to call *Sailor on Horseback*. But his wife of eleven years, Charmian, took time to record her memories of him, published in a two-volume set titled *The Book of Jack London*:

One passage said:

> *He never wore nor waved a flag; his flags, his colours, were in his eyes, streamed from his pen, and waved from his printed page. Everyone who tried to understand him was better for it. When persons say, "I never met him," I can only return, "I am*

London holds one of the piglets from his farm in this photograph taken six days before he died.

sorry." If it was a privilege to know his work, it was a greater privilege to know himself, if ever so slightly, for he was greater than his work.[3]

The volume of work he published is incredible. He wrote at least one thousand words a day for seventeen years and sold almost everything he wrote. He gave the world stories on a variety of subjects, including hoboing, prizefighting, seafaring, alcoholism, and human and animal psychology. His writing has affected readers in many ways.

Jack London was a human being, a product of his time, with flaws like the rest of the human race. His struggles were great, his accomplishments many. London's disappointments were heartbreaking, his triumphs glorious.

He wrote:

I think that the greatest thing in each man's life is his own personal struggle to live, to survive, to succeed, in spite of all the odds against him. And the test . . . is all in that struggle, and how he handles himself. Does he whimper, does he whine? Is he dishonest, a coward? Then I doubt he can make it. But if he handles himself like a loyal and an honest man, then I think he's got every chance.[4]

The life of Jack London illustrates the importance of the struggle and the importance of hope. Many individuals and institutions, including his family members, have dedicated themselves to keeping his memory alive. His home state of California pays special tribute to him in many ways, including the Jack London Bookstore and Research Center and the Jack

The House of Happy Walls at Jack London State Historic Park in Glen Ellen, California, a memorial to Jack London, stands near the park entrance.

London State Historic Park, both in Glen Ellen, Sonoma County, California.

In the park the concrete block silos and the piggery, now affectionately known as "The Pig Palace," still stand. Visitors can walk the trails he rode and see the lake where Jack London swam. They can admire the cottage and feel the presence of the man who wrote there. They can visit the grave site, the ruins of the Wolf House, and the museum called the House of Happy Walls where London memorabilia are displayed.

One visitor, Anthony Acerrano, first read *The Call of the Wild* when he was in fourth grade. Years later, he journeyed to Jack London's grave site in Glen Ellen and described London's appeal to him:

> *Written language had never excited me to such a pitch, nor had anything seemed so alluring and beautiful and free as the wild land where Buck roamed and wolves sang to the moon. I read Buck's story every year after that until high school, and was amazed at the way the tale grew wider and deeper with each reading. This was one small fire among millions that Jack London had kindled in his readers; and it is partially this debt to him, this gratitude, which brings me to peer at his gravestone on a little knoll in California.*[5]

London's wooden desk is on display at Jack London State Historic Park.

At this grave site amid the trees Jack London loved, it is easy to remember his legacy. He was the writer who explored the land, the sea, and the heart. He was the little boy who loved books, and these books opened up new worlds for him. His books continue to open up new worlds for others.

Chronology

1876— Born in San Francisco, California, on January 12.

1878— London family moves to Oakland, California.

1891— Graduates eighth grade from the Cole Grammar School; works at Hickmott's Cannery; becomes an oyster pirate on San Francisco Bay; buys his first boat, *Razzle Dazzle*.

1892— Serves as a deputy patrolman for the California Fish Patrol.

1893— Joins the crew of the *Sophia Sutherland*, a sealing schooner; his "Story of a Typhoon Off the Coast of Japan" wins first prize in a contest sponsored by the *San Francisco Morning Call*.

1894— Arrested for vagrancy and serves thirty days in the Erie County Penitentiary; returns to Oakland.

1895— Attends Oakland High School.

1897— Leaves the University of California after one semester; works in the Belmont Academy laundry; joins the Klondike gold rush; father dies.

1898— Returns from the Klondike; works on his writing; sells his first story, "To the Man on Trail."

1899— "To the Man on Trail" is published in the *Overland Monthly*.

1900— Marries Bessie May Maddern; *The Son of the Wolf* is published.

1901— First daughter, Joan, is born; runs unsuccessfully for mayor of Oakland.

1902— Lives in the East End of London for two months to research *The People of the Abyss*; second daughter, Becky, is born.

1903— *The Call of the Wild* is published; falls in love with Charmian Kittredge; separates from his wife, Bessie London; buys a sailboat, the *Spray*.

1904— Serves as a correspondent in Korea during the Russo-Japanese War; wife files for divorce.

1905— Second unsuccessful bid for mayor of Oakland; buys land in Glen Ellen, California, the start of his Beauty Ranch; divorce is official; marries Charmian Kittredge.

1906— Construction of the *Snark* begins for his planned cruise around the world; reports on the San Francisco earthquake; *White Fang* is published.

1907— Begins his cruise around the world on the *Snark*.

1908— Is hospitalized in Sydney, Australia.

1909— Returns to Oakland; *Martin Eden* is published.

1910— Daughter Joy is born but dies two days later; expands Beauty Ranch to nearly 1,000 acres.

1911— Drives four-horse wagon on 1,340-mile trip to Oregon and back; moves from Wake Robin Lodge to Ranch House; construction on Wolf House begins.

1912— Sails on *Dirigo* for five-month voyage to Seattle around Cape Horn.

1913— Wolf House destroyed by fire.

1914— Reports on the Mexican Revolution for *Collier's*.

1916— Suffers from uremia and rheumatism; dies on November 22 in Glen Ellen, California.

Books by Jack London

A Selected List of Fiction

The Son of the Wolf, 1900
The God of His Fathers, 1901
Children of the Frost, 1902
The Cruise of the Dazzler, 1902
The Kempton-Wace Letters, 1903
The Call of the Wild, 1903
The People of the Abyss, 1903
The Faith of Men, 1904
The Sea Wolf, 1904
War of the Classes, 1905
Tales of the Fish Patrol, 1905
White Fang, 1906
Love of Life, 1907
The Road, 1907
Martin Eden, 1909
Burning Daylight, 1910
The Cruise of the Snark, 1911
Smoke Bellew, 1912
John Barleycorn, 1913
The Valley of the Moon, 1913
The Mutiny of the Elsinore, 1914
The Star Rover, 1915

Suggested Collections

Jack London: American Rebel—A Collection of His Social Writings Together with an Extensive Study of the Man and His Times, edited by Philip S. Foner. New York: Citadel Press, 1947.

Jack London Reports [essays and newspaper articles], edited by King Hendricks and Irving Shepard. New York: Doubleday, 1970.

The Letters of Jack London, edited by Earle Labor, Robert C. Leitz, III, and I. Milo Shepard. 3 vols. Stanford, California: Stanford University Press, 1988.

The Complete Short Stories of Jack London, edited by Earle Labor, Robert C. Leitz, III, and I. Milo Shepard. 3 vols. Stanford, California: Stanford University Press, 1993.

Chapter Notes

Chapter 1. "Thirty Days"

1. Jack London, *The Road* (Santa Barbara, Calif.: Peregrine Smith, Inc., 1970; originally published 1907), pp. 77–80.

2. Ibid., pp. 81, 95.

3. Jack London, "What Life Means to Me," in *Jack London: American Rebel—A Collection of His Social Writings Together with an Extensive Study of the Man and His Times*, ed. Philip S. Foner (New York: The Citadel Press, 1947, 1964), p. 395.

4. London, *The Road*, p. 97.

5. King Hendricks and Irving Shepard, eds., *Jack London Reports: War Correspondence, Sports Articles, and Miscellaneous Writings* (New York: Doubleday and Company, 1970), p. xi.

6. Jack London, "How I Became a Socialist," in *Jack London: American Rebel*, ed. Foner, p. 364.

7. Hendricks and Shepard, p. xi.

8. London, "How I Became a Socialist," p. 395.

9. Russ Kingman, *A Pictorial Biography of Jack London* (Middletown, Calif.: David Rejl, 1979), p. 116.

10. *The Bulletin* (San Francisco), December 2, 1916, (Jack London Collection, Henry E. Huntington Library, San Marino, California).

Chapter 2. Early Lessons

1. Charmian London, *The Book of Jack London* (New York: Century Co., 1921), vol. 1, p. 35.

2. Ibid., p. 29.

3. Jack London, *John Barleycorn or Alcoholic Memoirs* (Esparto, Calif.: Lexicos, 1997; originally published 1913), p. 8.

4. Ibid., p. 9.

5. Ibid., p. 19.

6. Charmian London, p. 52.

7. "Eight Great Factors of Literary Success," Document 403094, Jack London Collection, Henry E. Huntington Library, San Marino, California.

8. Letter from Jack London to Ina Coolbrith, December 13, 1906. Copy of clippings in the Ina Coolbrith scrapbook, Oakland Public Library; copy obtained from the Jack London Research Center, Glen Ellen, California.

9. Charmian London, p. 56.

10. Jack London, p. 31.

11. Ibid., pp. 31–32.

12. Clarice Stasz, *American Dreamers: Charmian and Jack London* (New York: St. Martin's Press, 1988), p. 42.

13. Jack London, p. 32.

14. Jack London, *The Cruise of the Dazzler* (Oakland: Star Rover, 1981; originally published 1902), pp. 166–167.

15. Jack London, *John Barleycorn*, p. 47.

16. Jack London, *Jack London by Himself* (Grand Rapids, Mich.: Wolf House Books, 1973), p. 1.

17. Jack London, *John Barleycorn*, p. 39.

18. Ibid., p. 51.

19. Russ Kingman, *A Pictorial Biography of Jack London* (Middletown, Calif.: David Rejl, 1979), p. 39.

20. Jack London, *Jack London by Himself*, p. 3.

21. Jack London, *Tales of the Fish Patrol* (Oakland, Calif.: Star Rover House, 1982; originally published 1905), pp. 177–178.

22. Jack London, *John Barleycorn*, p. 67.

23. Ibid., p. 62.

24. Kingman, p. 40.

Chapter 3. Adventure by Sea, Adventure by Land

1. Charmian London, *The Book of Jack London* (New York: Century Co., 1921), vol. 1, p. 114.

2. Ibid., p. 362.

3. Ibid., p. 130.

4. Charmian London, *Jack London* (London, England: Mills and Boon, Ltd., 1921), vol. 1, p. 143. [*Author's note*: This British edition, *Jack London*, contains some information not included in the American edition, *The Book of Jack London*. Both editions were consulted in researching this book.]

5. Joan London, *Jack London and His Times, an Unconventional Biography* (New York: Doubleday, Doran & Company, Inc., 1939), p. 66.

6. Earle Labor, Robert C. Leitz, III, and I. Milo Shepard, eds., *Short Stories of Jack London*, authorized one-volume ed. (New York: Macmillan, 1990), p. 6. (Story originally printed in the *San Francisco Morning Call*, November 12, 1893, and published by Macmillan, 1927).

7. Jack London, *John Barleycorn or Alcoholic Memoirs* (Esparto, Calif.: Lexicos, 1997; originally published 1913), p. 102.

8. Ibid., p. 104.

9. Ibid., p. 106.

10. Jack London, *The Road* (Santa Barbara, Calif.: Peregrine Smith, Inc., 1970; originally published 1907), p. 39.

11. Ibid., p. 19.

12. Jack London, *Jack London by Himself* (Grand Rapids, Mich.: Wolf House Books, 1973), p. 5.

13. Excerpt from the *San Francisco Chronicle*, February 16, 1896, in Alex Kershaw, *Jack London: A Life* (New York: St. Martin's Press, 1997), p. 45.

14. *The Bulletin* (San Francisco), December 2, 1916, p. 1 (Jack London Collection, Henry E. Huntington Library, San Marino, California).

Chapter 4. ". . . Like a Dry Sponge"

1. Charmian London, *The Book of Jack London* (New York: Century Co., 1921), vol. 1, p. 192.

2. Ibid., p. 193.

3. Georgia Loring Bamford, *The Mystery of Jack London, Some of His Friends, Also a Few Letters* (Oakland, Calif.: Georgia Loring Bamford, 1931), p. 21.

4. James Sisson III, ed., *Jack London's Articles and Short Stories in The Aegis* (Oakland, Calif.: Star Rover House, 1980), p. 20. (First published in *The Aegis* on March 1, 1895.)

5. Joan London, *Jack London and His Times* (New York: Doubleday, Doran & Company, Inc., 1939), p. 128.

6. Ibid., p. 134.

7. Russ Kingman, *A Pictorial Biography of Jack London* (Middletown, Calif.: David Rejl, 1979), p. 67.

8. Ibid., p. 68.

9. Jack London, *John Barleycorn or Alcoholic Memoirs* (Esparto, Calif.: Lexicos, 1997; originally published 1907), p. 117.

Chapter 5. The Klondike

1. Charmian London, *The Book of Jack London* (New York: Century Co., 1921), vol. 1, p. 227.

2. Russ Kingman, *A Pictorial Biography of Jack London* (Middletown, Calif.: David Rejl, 1979), p. 76.

3. Franklin Walker, *Jack London and the Klondike: The Genesis of an American Writer* (San Marino, Calif.: Huntington Library, 1966, 1994), p. 102.

4. Andrew Sinclair, *Jack: A Biography of Jack London* (New York: Harper and Row, 1977), pp. 47–48.

5. Jack London, "A Day's Lodging," in Earle Labor, Robert C. Leitz, III, and I. Milo Shepard, eds., *The Complete Short Stories of Jack London* (Stanford: Stanford University Press, 1993), vol. 2, p. 1088.

6. Kingman, p. 78.

7. Ibid., p. 80.

8. Charmian London, p. 236.

9. Ibid., p. 253.

10. Kingman, p. 91.

11. Charmian London, pp. 253–254.

Chapter 6. Learning the Craft

1. Earle Labor, Robert C. Leitz, III, and I. Milo Shepard, eds., *The Letters of Jack London, Volume One: 1896–1905* (Stanford: Stanford University Press, 1988), p. 18.

2. Jack London, "To the Man on Trail," in Earle Labor, Robert C. Leitz, III, and I. Milo Shepard, eds., *The Complete Short Stories of Jack London* (Stanford: Stanford University Press, 1993), vol. 1, p. 156.

3. Joan London, *Jack London and His Times* (New York: Doubleday, Doran & Company, Inc., 1939), p. 194.

4. Russ Kingman, *A Pictorial Biography of Jack London* (Middletown, Calif.: David Rejl, 1979), p. 85.

5. Ibid., p. 104.

6. Andrew Sinclair, *Jack: A Biography of Jack London* (New York: Harper and Row, 1977), p. 73.

7. Franklin Walker, *Jack London and the Klondike: The Genesis of an American Writer* (San Marino, Calif.: Huntington Library, 1966, 1994), pp. 207–208.

8. Jack London, *Martin Eden* (New York: Holt, Rhinehart & Winston, 1970; originally published 1909), p. 111.

9. Kingman, p. 101.

10. Joan London, p. 196.

11. James I. McClintock, *Jack London's Strong Truths: A Study of His Short Stories* (East Lansing, Mich.: Michigan State University Press, 1975, 1997), p. 7.

12. Labor, Leitz, and Shepard, *The Letters of Jack London*, p. 240.

13. Walker, p. 226.

14. Joan London, p. 256.

15. Charmian London, *The Book of Jack London*, (New York: Century Co., 1921), vol. 1, p. 378.

16. Jack London, *The People of the Abyss* (New York: Lawrence Hill Books, 1995; originally published 1903), pp. 227–229.

17. Alex Kershaw, *Jack London: A Life* (New York: St. Martin's Press, 1997), p. 119.

18. Jack London, *The People of the Abyss*, pp. 212–213.

19. Labor, Leitz, and Shepard, *The Letters of Jack London*, p. 306.

20. Ibid., p. 307.

21. Ibid., p. 352.

22. Jack London, *The Call of the Wild* (New York: Oxford University Press, 1990; originally published 1903), p. 29.

23. Kingman, p. 116.

Chapter 7. Jack and Charmian

1. King Hendricks and Irving Shepard, eds., *Jack London Reports: War Correspondence, Sports Articles, and Miscellaneous Writing* (New York: Doubleday and Company, 1970), p. 15.

2. Andrew Sinclair, *Jack: A Biography of Jack London* (New York: Harper and Row, 1977), p. 105.

3. Hendricks and Shepard, p. 120.

4. Russ Kingman, *A Pictorial Biography of Jack London* (Middletown, Calif.: David Rejl, 1979), p. 136.

5. Broadside JLB 63, Henry E. Huntington Library, San Marino, California.

6. Joan London, *Jack London and His Times* (New York: Doubleday, Doran & Company, Inc., 1939), p. 302.

7. Ibid., p. 297.

8. Ibid., p. 303.

9. Kingman, p. 155.

10. Ephemera Collection Box 522, Henry E. Huntington Library, San Marino, California.

11. Charmian London, *The Book of Jack London* (New York: Century Co., 1921), vol. 2, p. 28.

12. Ibid., p. 160.

13. Ibid., p. 150.

14. Ibid., p. 143.

15. Ibid., p. 137.

16. Jack London, "The Story of an Eyewitness," in Elizabeth C. O'Daly and Egbert W. Nieman, eds., *Adventures for Readers* (New York: Harcourt Brace Jovanovich, Inc., 1973), p. 508.

17. Charmian London, *The Log of the Snark* (New York: Macmillan, 1916), pp. 79–80.

18. Earle Labor, Robert C. Leitz, III, and I. Milo Shepard, eds., *The Letters of Jack London, Volume Two: 1906–1912* (Stanford: Stanford University Press), p. 768.

19. Kingman, p. 201.

20. Hendricks and Shepard, pp. 262–263.

21. Charmian London, *The Book of Jack London*, p. 189.

Chapter 8. The Final Years

1. Ephemera: Ranch Notes Box 582 A-F, Henry E. Huntington Library, San Marino, California.

2. Charmian London, *The Book of Jack London* (New York: Century Co., 1921), vol. 2, p. 269.

3. Russ Kingman, *A Pictorial Biography of Jack London* (Middletown, Calif.: David Rejl, 1979), p. 229.

4. London, p. 318.

5. Charmian London, *Jack London* (London, England: Mills and Boon, Ltd., 1921), vol. 2, p. 238.

6. Earl Labor, Robert C. Leitz, III, and I. Milo Shepard, eds., *The Letters of Jack London: Volume Three: 1913–1916* (Stanford: Stanford University Press, 1988), p. 1206, n. 2.

7. Ibid., p. 1212.

8. London, *The Book of Jack London*, p. 262.

9. Clarice Stasz, *American Dreamers: Charmian and Jack London* (New York: St. Martin's Press, 1988), p. 222.

10. Earl Labor, Robert C. Leitz, III, and I. Milo Shepard, eds., *The Letters of Jack London: Volume Two: 1906–1912* (Stanford: Stanford University Press, 1988), p. 971.

11. *The Bulletin* (San Francisco), November 18, 1916, Broadside JLB #16, Henry E. Huntington Library, San Marino, California.

12. Stasz, p. 316.

13. Labor, Leitz, and Shepard, *Volume Three*, p. 1604.

14. London, *The Book of Jack London*, pp. 392–393.

15. London, *Jack London*, p. 384.

Chapter 9. The London Legacy

1. Charmian London, *The Book of Jack London* (New York: Century Co., 1921), vol. 2, p. 394.

2. Ibid., p. 395.

3. Ibid., p. 344.

4. William Kushner, *Jack London: A Life of Adventure, Guidance Associates Teacher's Guide* (Mt. Kisco, N.Y.: Guidance Associates, Inc., 1969), p. 26.

5. Anthony Acerrano, *Sports Afield*, December 1983, pp. 56, 58.

Further Reading

Dyer, Daniel. *Jack London: A Biography*. New York: Scholastic, 1997.

Kershaw, Alex. *Jack London: A Life*. New York: St. Martin's Press, 1997.

Kingman, Russ. *Jack London: A Definitive Chronology*. Middletown, Calif.: David Rejl, 1992.

———. *A Pictorial Biography of Jack London*. Middletown, Calif.: David Rejl, 1979. [Also published as *A Pictorial Life of Jack London*. New York: Crown, 1979.]

Labor, Earle, and Jeanne Campbell Reeseman. *Jack London*. Revised edition. New York: Twayne Publishers, 1994.

London, Charmian Kittredge. *The Book of Jack London*. 2 vols. New York: Century, 1921. [Also published as *Jack London*. London, England: Mills and Boon, Ltd., 1921.]

———. *The Log of the Snark*. New York: Macmillan, 1915.

London, Joan. *Jack London and His Times*. New York: Doubleday, 1939. Reprint, with a new introduction by the author, Seattle: University of Washington Press, 1968.

McClintock, James I. *Jack London's Strong Truths: A Study of His Short Stories*. East Lansing, Mich.: Michigan State University Press, 1997. Originally published as *White Logic: Jack London's Short Stories*. Grand Rapids, Mich.: Wolf House Books, 1975.

Nuernberg, Susan, ed. *The Critical Response to Jack London*. Westport, Conn.: Greenwood Press, 1995.

Schroeder, Alan. *Jack London*. New York: Chelsea House, 1992.

Stasz, Clarice. *American Dreamers: Charmian and Jack London*. New York: St. Martin's Press, 1988.

Tavernier-Courbin, Jacqueline. *The Call of the Wild: A Naturalistic Romance*. New York: Twayne Publishers, 1994.

Walker, Franklin. *Jack London and the Klondike: The Genesis of an American Writer*. San Marino, Calif.: Huntington Library, 1966.

Booklets

Haughey, Homer L., and Connie Kale Johnson. *Jack London Ranch Album*. Stockton: Heritage Publishing Company, 1995. (Available from the Jack London State Historic Park Bookstore.)

McKee, Martha L. *Jack London in California: A Guide*. Ketchum, Ind.: Computer Lab, 1995. (Available from the Jack London Bookstore in Glen Ellen, California.)

Video

California's Gold #502 "Jack London." Funded by Wells Fargo. Available from Valley of the Moon Natural History Association, 2400 London Ranch Road, Glen Ellen, CA 95442 <http://parks.sonoma.net>

Other Resources

Jack London Book Store
Jack London Research Center
P.O. Box 337 (14300 Arnold Drive)
Glen Ellen, CA 95442
(707) 996-2888

Jack London State Historic Park
2400 London Ranch Road
Glen Ellen, California 95442
(707) 938-5216

Valley of the Moon Natural History Association
2400 London Ranch Road
Glen Ellen, CA 95442
<http://parks.sonoma.net/orderform.htm>

This organization still celebrates Jack London's birthday each January. It supports school programs and writing contests:

Jack London Foundation
P.O. Box 337
14300 Arnold Drive
Glen Ellen, California 95442

Winnie Kingman at the Jack London Bookstore and Research Center in Glen Ellen, California.

This international nonprofit organization promotes study of the life and works of Jack London:

The Jack London Society
Contact: Professor Jeanne Campbell Reeseman
University of Texas
San Antonio, TX 78249

A replica of the *Snark*, built by Warren and Toby Watson, is located at the Maritime Museum in San Francisco next to Fisherman's Wharf.

The Jack London Museum and Jack London Village are located on the Oakland, California, waterfront.

Internet Addresses

The Jack London Collection
<http://sunsite.berkeley.edu/London/>

Jack London's Ranch Album™
<http://www.geocities.com/~jacklondons/intro.html>

Jack London State Historic Park
<http://parks.sonoma.net/JLPark.html>

Related Links to Jack London and Glen Ellen
<http://www.jacklondon.com/jacklinks.htm>

Index